Teens and Cheating

Teenage Problems

ReferencePoint Press®

San Diego, CA

Other books in the Compact Research Teenage Problems set:

Teenage Alcoholism
Teenage Dropouts
Teenage Drug Abuse
Teenage Eating Disorders
Teenage Sex and Pregnancy
Teenage Suicide
Teen Violence
Teens and Stress
Teens: Cutting and Self-Injury

*For a complete list of titles please visit www.referencepointpress.com.

Teens and Cheating

Peggy J. Parks

Teenage Problems

ReferencePoint
Press®

San Diego, CA

About the Author

Peggy J. Parks holds a bachelor of science degree from Aquinas College in Grand Rapids, Michigan, where she graduated magna cum laude. An author who has written more than one hundred educational books for children and young adults, Parks lives in Muskegon, Michigan, a town that she says inspires her writing because of its location on the shores of Lake Michigan.

© 2015 ReferencePoint Press, Inc.
Printed in the United States

For more information, contact:
ReferencePoint Press, Inc.
PO Box 27779
San Diego, CA 92198
www.ReferencePointPress.com

Picture credits:
Cover credit: iStockphoto.com and Thinkstock/Comstock Images
Maury Aaseng: 32–34, 46–47, 60–62, 74–76
Thinkstock Images: 14, 17

LIBRARY OF CONGRESS CATALOGING-IN-PUBLICATION DATA

Teens and cheating / by Peggy J Parks.
    pages cm. -- (Compact research series)
  Includes bibliographical references and index.
  ISBN 978-1-60152-766-0 (hardback) -- ISBN 1-60152-766-7 (hardback)
1. Cheating (Education)--Juvenile literature. 2. Teenagers--Attitudes--Juvenile literature. I. Title.
  LB3609.P354   2016
  808.02'5--dc23
                                             2014040765

Contents

Foreword

As modern civilization continues to evolve, its ability to create, store, distribute, and access information expands exponentially. The explosion of information from all media continues to increase at a phenomenal rate. By 2020 some experts predict the worldwide information base will double every seventy-three days. While access to diverse sources of information and perspectives is paramount to any democratic society, information alone cannot help people gain knowledge and understanding. Information must be organized and presented clearly and succinctly in order to be understood. The challenge in the digital age becomes not the creation of information, but how best to sort, organize, enhance, and present information.

ReferencePoint Press developed the *Compact Research* series with this challenge of the information age in mind. More than any other subject area today, researching current issues can yield vast, diverse, and unqualified information that can be intimidating and overwhelming for even the most advanced and motivated researcher. The *Compact Research* series offers a compact, relevant, intelligent, and conveniently organized collection of information covering a variety of current topics ranging from illegal immigration and deforestation to diseases such as anorexia and meningitis.

The series focuses on three types of information: objective single-author narratives, opinion-based primary source quotations, and facts and statistics. The clearly written objective narratives provide context and reliable background information. Primary source quotes are carefully selected and cited, exposing the reader to differing points of view, and facts and statistics sections aid the reader in evaluating perspectives. Presenting these key types of information creates a richer, more balanced learning experience.

For better understanding and convenience, the series enhances information by organizing it into narrower topics and adding design features that make it easy for a reader to identify desired content. For example, in *Compact Research: Illegal Immigration*, a chapter covering the economic impact of illegal immigration has an objective narrative explaining the various ways the economy is impacted, a balanced section of numerous primary source quotes on the topic, followed by facts and full-color illustrations to encourage evaluation of contrasting perspectives.

The ancient Roman philosopher Lucius Annaeus Seneca wrote, "It is quality rather than quantity that matters." More than just a collection of content, the *Compact Research* series is simply committed to creating, finding, organizing, and presenting the most relevant and appropriate amount of information on a current topic in a user-friendly style that invites, intrigues, and fosters understanding.

Teens and Cheating at a Glance

Scope of Cheating

Cheating refers to everything from texting test answers to classmates or copying someone's homework to breaking the rules of a game in order to win.

How Widespread

According to the New York University (NYU) Child Study Center, 75 percent of teens have cheated on tests, homework, or other assignments.

Gender

Most experts say teenage boys and girls cheat about equally, although some surveys show that cheating is more common among boys.

Technology and Cheating

Smartphones, the Internet, and other forms of technology have made cheating easier than ever before, and some experts say this has led to an increase in cheating.

Plagiarism

Claiming someone else's work as one's own is known as plagiarism, and experts say this type of cheating is soaring because of the ease of copying documents from websites.

Why Teens Cheat

Reasons for cheating range from pressure to achieve high grades and get into a good college to peer pressure and diminishing ethics.

Effects

Ethics specialists warn that teens who continue to get away with cheating will become indifferent to it, lose their sense of pride in accomplishments from hard work, and potentially develop unethical behavior as adults.

Solutions

Recommendations include less emphasis on grades and testing, greater emphasis on ethics, implementing honor code systems, and banning cell phones from schools.

Overview

❝There have always been struggling students who cheat to survive. But more and more, there are students at the top who cheat to thrive.❞

—Donald L. McCabe, a retired professor from Rutgers University who is a well-known authority on ethics and academic cheating.

❝Cheating is not solely the fault of our students or the declining ethical standards of the millennial generation, but a product of our testing-oriented and performance-obsessed culture.❞

—Jessica Lahey, an English, Latin, and writing teacher from New Hampshire, who is also an author and contributing writer for the *New York Times* and the *Atlantic*.

Years ago a common belief among educators and administrators was that teens who cheated were those who had the hardest time in school. As these young people became overwhelmed and fell further and further behind, many viewed cheating as their last chance to avoid flunking out. That generalization is not accurate today, as clinical psychologist Laura Kastner writes: "Back in the day (the dark ages of our youth) it was the struggling student who was most likely to venture to the dark side of cheating. Not these days. Now, countless high-performing students are joining the cheating throngs, claiming they have to resort to deception and dishonesty to compete in the cutthroat, competitive college-admissions game."[1]

One notorious example of cheating among high-performing students took place in 2012 at Stuyvesant High School in New York City. One of the nation's most elite schools, Stuyvesant is well known for attracting the best and brightest young people. Each year thousands of teens compete for about eight hundred coveted freshman spots, and acceptance is solely based on how high they score on an entrance exam. Stuyvesant's SAT scores are among the highest of any school in the United States. Yet even with such impeccable credentials, Stuyvesant's reputation was seriously damaged because of an incident that journalist Robert Kolker calls "the most brazen feat of cheating in the illustrious school's 107-year history."[2]

Stuyvesant Scandal

It happened in June 2012, when juniors at Stuyvesant High School were taking state standardized tests called Regents Examinations. On the night of June 12, a popular student named Nayeem Ahsan sent a group text to 140 classmates. He told them to expect a text from him the next day while he was taking his Regents exam in physics, a subject at which he excelled. As promised, on June 13 Ahsan finished his exam and surreptitiously used his iPhone to snap pictures of the completed fifteen-page booklet, which he texted to the group. In return, classmates who were more proficient in history and Spanish would send Ahsan photos of their answers to use while he was taking exams. "He was the point person on this exam," says Kolker. "Others would play that role for subjects they excelled in."[3] The scheme was working exactly as Ahsan had planned—until he got caught. He had no idea that a classmate had anonymously e-mailed principal Stanley Teitel to alert him about the cheating plan, and Teitel had set up an internal sting operation to catch Ahsan in the act.

> " One notorious example of cheating among high-performing students took place in 2012 at Stuyvesant High School in New York City. "

On June 18, 2012, Ahsan was taking his Spanish exam (and receiving the promised answers via text) when Teitel walked into the room accompanied by several other administrators. He stopped in front of Ahsan's desk and asked if he had a cell phone, to which Ahsan replied that he did. Teitel then ordered him to hand over his phone, and after a moment of futile protest Ahsan did so. As he was being escorted to the office, Ahsan tried to remain calm but that proved to be impossible. Contained within his phone was all the incriminating evidence Teitel needed: the texts Ahsan had sent and received, names of students with whom he had been exchanging information, and a record of every exam for which Ahsan had shared answers since the beginning of the school term.

Word traveled fast about the incident, which the media dubbed the Stuyvesant cheating scandal. Over the subsequent months the New York City Department of Education conducted an investigation, which resulted in Ahsan being expelled and nearly seventy other students being suspended. Afterward, many students spoke out on behalf of Stuyvesant, saying they hoped its stellar reputation could eventually be restored. "We all want to prove that Stuy is one of the top schools in the city," says Rachel Makombo, who entered Stuyvesant as a freshman in the fall of 2012. "We don't want to be looked at as a cheating school."[4]

A Word with Many Meanings

Cheating can take many forms. The Nemours Foundation, a children's health organization, defines cheating as "when a person misleads, deceives, or acts dishonestly on purpose."[5] Along with cheating on homework and tests, this may involve stealing a classmate's idea for a science project; cheating at games; copying a document from a website and claiming that it is one's own original work, which is known as plagiarism; or cheating on one's boyfriend or girlfriend by secretly being involved with someone else.

Another form of cheating is the use of performance-enhancing drugs in order to be stronger or faster than the competition. These drugs may include anabolic steroids, stimulants such as amphetamines, and synthetic human growth hormone (HGH), among others. According to a study released in July 2014 by the Partnership for Drug-Free Kids, there was a significant increase in the reported lifetime use of HGH among teenagers between 2012 and 2013. The study found that in 2013, 11 percent of teens in ninth through twelfth grades reported using the substance at some point during their lives without a prescription, which is more than double the 5 percent reported in 2012. Use of HGH was found to be greatest among African American teens (15 percent), followed by 13 percent of Hispanic teens and 9 percent of Caucasian teens.

Contradictory Perspectives

Surveys have shown that teenagers have a variety of different perspectives about cheating, from believing that it is always wrong to finding reasons to justify it. The various opinions teens have about cheating were revealed in November 2012, when the Josephson Institute of Ethics published its biennial report on the ethics of high school students in the United States. More than twenty-three thousand ninth through twelfth graders participated in the survey and responded to numerous statements about ethics-related issues. For instance, 99 percent of the teens said they think it is important to be a person of good character; 96 percent said they think it is important that people trust them; and 95 percent said that trust and honesty are essential in business and the workplace.

> **Studies have consistently shown that a large percentage of high school students have cheated in some way.**

Yet as strong as their opinions were about those ethics-related issues, responses to other statements proved to be somewhat contradictory. For instance, 36 percent of the teens agreed that people sometimes have to lie or cheat to succeed; 15 percent agreed that cheating is okay if others are doing it; and 57 percent said they think that successful people do whatever is needed to succeed even if others view their actions as cheating.

How Widespread Is Cheating Among Teens?

Studies have consistently shown that a large percentage of high school students have cheated in some way. In the 2012 Josephson Institute of Ethics study, for example, more than half of participants said they had cheated during a test at school, with 28 percent of those teens having cheated two or more times. Regarding homework assignments, three-fourths of the teens said they had copied someone else's work. Similar statistics are offered by the NYU Child Study Center, which writes: "Among current high school students, 75 percent admit to cheating on tests, homework, and other assignments. Fifty percent have cheated on exams during the past year, and 34 percent have cheated on more than one test. One out of

Research shows that cheating on tests, homework, and other school assignments is not uncommon among high school students. In surveys some teens say they cheat because other students are doing it or because they simply do not see it as wrong.

every three students has used the Internet to plagiarize an assignment."[6]

In the aftermath of the June 2012 Stuyvesant High School cheating scandal, a number of people publicly shared their perspectives. For a September 2012 *New York Times* article, more than three dozen current and former Stuyvesant students and teachers said during interviews that such large-scale cheating incidents are rare at the school—but they also said that cheating in some form goes on every day. This had actually been revealed two months before the Ahsan cheating incident, during a survey conducted by Stuyvesant school newspaper staff. Of more than two thousand students interviewed, more than 72 percent said they had copied another student's homework. An estimated 90 percent of seniors said they had heard about test questions from other students before taking an exam. Stuyvesant alumnus Adam Schorin, who was editor in chief of the school newspaper at the time of the survey, said it showed a "widespread, fairly accurate portrayal of what's going on."[7]

Gender Differences?

Experts often disagree about the role of gender in terms of which teens choose to cheat. Some are of the opinion that boys are more inclined to cheat than girls, whereas others say both boys and girls cheat at about the same rate. The latter is the perspective of Denise Pope, who is senior lecturer at Stanford University's Graduate School of Education and co-founder of Challenge Success, an organization that works with schools and families to improve student well-being and engagement with learning. "We haven't found that there are discernible gender differences," says Pope. "Many assume that boys are more likely to cheat than girls because they're more competitive, but the research actually doesn't support that."[8]

> " Technology experts emphasize that the Internet and smartphones have made cheating easier than ever before. "

From responses during the 2012 Josephson Institute of Ethics study, however, boys appear to be more likely than girls to engage in dishonest behavior. For instance, when presented with the statement "A person has to lie or cheat sometimes in order to succeed," nearly half of boys agreed, compared with 28 percent of girls. And boys were twice as likely as girls to agree with the statement "It's not cheating if everyone is doing it." In response to the statement "It's not worth it to lie or cheat because it hurts your character,"[9] one out of five boys *disagreed*, compared with one out of ten girls.

How Has Technology Affected Teen Cheating?

There is no way to know with any certainty whether cheating has increased because of technology. But technology experts emphasize that the Internet and smartphones have made cheating easier than ever before. According to security technology company McAfee, 15 percent of people aged ten to twenty-three have cheated on a test using a mobile device and 11 percent have cheated on a test using a technique they read about online. McAfee security expert Robert Siciliano says that "technology has really added fuel to the fire" for cheating, and the practice now has a "whole new realm beyond writing information on your hand or arm."[10]

Ohio State University educational psychology professor Eric M. Anderman has extensively studied academic cheating. He agrees that technology has made it easier for students to cheat—and much less likely that they will be caught. "If you have 30 kids in a classroom, it's not easy to catch them," says Anderman. "There's only so much one person can do. The kids really can get away with it."[11]

The Plagiarism Plague

Plagiarism has been a problem for as long as the written word has existed. But because of the Internet and the ease of copying and pasting sentences, paragraphs, and even entire documents, plagiarism is soaring. "The means to commit plagiarism is much easier," says Chris Harrick, who is an executive with the Oakland, California technology firm Turnitin. "It's definitely a growing concern among educators."[12] During the 2012 Josephson Institute of Ethics survey, one-third of teens said they had copied an Internet document for a classroom assignment, and 16 percent of those had plagiarized two or more times.

One of the most widespread plagiarism tactics is using papers that are available online through what are known as paper or essay mills. This proved to be an eye-opening discovery for Heloise Pechan, a high school teacher in McHenry County, Illinois, who was initially elated when a student who had shown no interest in the class turned in a well-written, informative essay on the classic book *To Kill a Mockingbird*. But she had an uneasy feeling that something was not quite right, so Pechan typed the student's first sentence into Google and found that the entire paper had been taken from an essay mill. "I went from amazement and excitement to 'Oh my God' in the space of a half-second,"[13] says Pechan.

Why Do Teens Cheat?

Even though motives for cheating can vary widely from person to person, ethics experts say that there are some commonalities among teens. For instance, an excuse that is repeatedly given by students is the increasing amount of pressure to succeed academically and get into a good college. As one high school student bluntly states: "If you don't go to a good college, you are not going to do anything in life. I cheat, and I don't feel bad about it."[14]

Plagiarism is easier than ever before thanks to computers and the Internet. Some students cannot resist the temptation to copy and paste sentences, paragraphs, and even whole documents into their research papers or reports.

Surveys that examine cheating among high school students have often found that teens tend to place the blame on people or circumstances outside of themselves. In an August 2013 *Forbes* article, Stanford University public service and philanthropy experts Thomas Ehrlich and Ernestine Fu list the three most common excuses students give for cheating, and they all involve justifying it, blaming someone else, or minimizing the importance of what they have done: "It's no big deal," "I just got a little help—that's not really cheating," and "Everyone does it." Ehrlich and Fu write: "These excuses often accompany a student's pursuit of high grades or the desire to get into college or graduate school, which too often trumps their ethical judgments."[15]

The Contagion Factor

According to Virginia psychologist David A. Rettinger, even though students are usually aware that cheating is wrong and constitutes breaking the rules, most are still influenced by their peers and look to them for cues about what behaviors are acceptable. "Cheating is contagious,"[16] he says. Rettinger conducted his own study of 158 students, which revealed that the biggest predictor of cheating was having direct knowledge that others were cheating.

Even young people who are against cheating and have no intention of being involved in it may find it difficult to resist when all their peers are sharing information. For instance, students often form Facebook groups for the sole purpose of sharing information with each other. "Even students not trying to, end up cheating in ways," says Jenna Gavenman, a teen from California. She says that a student might click into Facebook with the best intentions, such as looking for help with one question, but then find that his or her classmates are sharing answers to everything. "I definitely think it does make it harder for kids who don't cheat,"[17] says Gavenman.

Negative Effects of Cheating

Ethics professionals say that the more young people cheat and get away with it, the easier it becomes to rationalize the behavior and keep cheating without guilt. In psychology this is known as desensitization. It refers to someone who is so often exposed to a situation, behavior, or object that he or she eventually becomes indifferent, or desensitized, to it. A California teen wrote anonymously about her changing attitude toward cheating in her high school's online magazine: "Honestly, who hasn't cheated before? I've done it so much that I don't feel bad about it anymore. I don't feel good, but I no longer hate myself for cheating."[18]

According to the NYU Child Study Center, the worst risk of repeated cheating is to young people's self-esteem and sense of competence. "Success is only worthwhile when it is based on true merit," the group writes. "If a grade is not as high as

> " Even young people who are against cheating and have no intention of being involved in it may find it difficult to resist when all their peers are sharing information. "

a student had hoped, there is immeasurable consolation in having made an honest effort. No matter the outcome, trying your best is its own reward."[19] There is also a longer-term risk of repeated cheating: It can potentially lead to unethical behavior as an adult. The NYU Child Study Center explains, "Cheating in school has also been linked to similar, unethical behaviors once young people are out in the 'real world.'

> " One preventive tactic that many education specialists strongly recommend is to reduce or eliminate the heavy emphasis on testing and grades. "

. . . Early habits and rationalizations can pave the way for potentially damaging decisions later in life. Many cheaters do get caught, both in school and in the real world, upending lives and ruining reputations."[20]

How Should Teen Cheating Be Addressed?

Cheating has proved to be a formidable problem; one that has been made worse by technology. It will not be an easy problem to solve. But experts say measures must be taken to curtail cheating and teach young people the importance of ethics and honesty. "All of us are in a position to have a real impact on school and college cheating," Ehrlich and Fu write. "We should do everything we can to minimize if not eliminate it."[21]

One preventive tactic that many education specialists strongly recommend is to reduce or eliminate the heavy emphasis on testing and grades. According to Challenge Success, research suggests that young people's perceptions of their classroom values and norms matter. "Specifically," the group explains, "students cheat more when they believe that grades and performance are valued in their classrooms, and they cheat less when they believe that learning and mastery are valued."[22]

No Easy Solutions

Unlike years ago, when students who cheated were assumed to be those who struggled the most, all kinds of teens cheat today—even those attending prestigious schools. From furnishing classmates with test answers via smartphone to plagiarizing essays from the Internet, cheating is a common occurrence among teens. Some experts say that it has gotten worse over time due to sophisticated technology, increased academic pressure, and growing apathy over whether or not cheating is wrong. Experts who specialize in cheating say that it is important to find creative ways of curbing it because there are innumerable risks involved if it continues unabated.

How Widespread Is Cheating Among Teens?

66**Students have cheated for as long as there have been schools, but by any measure, academic dishonesty is on the rise.**99

—Erika Christakis, an early childhood educator at the Yale University Child Study Center, and Nicholas A. Christakis, codirector of Yale's Institute for Network Science.

66**Indeed, the numbers are sobering, and the problem is widespread.**99

—Denise Pope, senior lecturer at Stanford University's Graduate School of Education and cofounder of the group Challenge Success, which works with schools and families to improve student well-being and engagement with learning.

During the 2012–2013 school year, when Giovanna Bishop was a junior at Grant High School in Portland, Oregon, she was taking an AP calculus class. The time was nearing for the final exam, and Bishop felt confident that she was ready for it. She had worked hard, studied a lot, and was carrying an A average in the class. Still, when a senior in her class asked if they could work together to prepare for the exam, Bishop agreed. She had no idea what she was getting into.

While she was working on solving calculus problems, Bishop became aware of something that stunned her. What she had thought was a study paper was actually a copy of the final exam, which her classmate had stolen from the math teacher's classroom. Bishop admits that once she was past the initial shock she felt somewhat torn, as she explains: "I thought, 'Oh great, what are we supposed to do,' but at the same time I was like 'OK, I guess it's kind of like a freebie.'"[23] She soon learned what a bad decision that was, because she and the other student were caught with the stolen exam. The "freebie" resulted in Bishop earning an automatic F on the final, and her classmate was suspended from school and received an F for the class.

A Pervasive Problem

Bishop felt horrible about her involvement in the cheating incident. She liked the class and admired the teacher, which made her feel even worse. "Lesson learned," she says. "Once you go through something like that you never want to do it again."[24] Yet she acknowledges that it can be hard for students to make the right decision when they get caught up in a culture of cheating. Bishop also admits that if she had not gotten caught, she probably would have gone ahead and taken the exam even though she had seen it beforehand.

The story of the stolen exam was featured in a March 2013 article in the high school news magazine, *Grant Magazine*. A number of students besides Bishop were interviewed for the article, and their opinions about cheating varied widely. One Grant High student, Jonzanae Johnson, spoke about how common cheating is at her school. "It's something that we just do," says Johnson. "You always know that if you don't have the answers, there's a friend that you can get the answer from. Everyone knows it's an option. It's something we depend on."[25] In a survey conducted by *Grant Magazine* staff, 96 percent of Grant High students said they had seen someone cheat or plagiarize at school. Of the teens who admitted that they themselves have cheated, fewer than 15 percent were ever caught. When asked what methods students used to cheat, the list included copying out of each other's notebooks, writing notes on their hands, using their smartphones to search online for answers to test questions, and plagiarizing papers from the Internet.

As for the Grant High teens who do not cheat but have observed oth-

> **Bishop felt horrible about her involvement in the cheating incident.**

ers cheating, they made it clear they would never tell on their classmates. "I can't imagine anyone ever going up to a teacher and being like, 'This person's cheating,'" says Grant High student Annie Willis. "Automatically, you would [be] labeled."[26] This may be the accepted norm among teens. But according to teachers and administrators, it is exactly the sort of thing that promotes a culture of cheating. Another concern is that it reinforces that cheating is acceptable and there are no repercussions for partaking in it.

Seaside Scandal

A 2013 cheating scandal at Corona del Mar High School in Newport Beach has shaken that Southern California community. A January 29, 2014, *Los Angeles Times* article describes the school as having "earned a reputation as one of the state's top public schools." The article adds: "Living in a seaside enclave of quaint old homes and cliff-top mansions, the school's students benefit from private tutors and their parents expect them to go on to elite universities." But the school's stellar reputation was tarnished by what the newspaper describes as "an ugly cheating scandal"[27] that resulted in eleven students being expelled.

School officials and police say that the cheating scheme was devised by a twenty-eight-year-old private tutor who got students to install a device on the computers of certain teachers. The device, called a keylogger, made it possible to monitor keystrokes and change students' grades and also gain access to English, science, and history exams. The scheme was discovered when a teacher noticed the changed grades and alerted administrators, who called police. Officials traced the scheme back to the tutor, who fled but was arrested in October 2014. The school board decision to expel the students who were accused of taking part in the scheme elicited both support and opposition. Skyler Gullick, a sophomore at Corona del Mar High School, told members of the school board that

> " The cheating scheme was devised by a twenty-eight-year-old private tutor who got students to install a device on the computers of certain teachers. "

she supported their decision. "It's a really serious crime," says Gullick. "I don't think they knew how serious it was."[28]

A Troubling Trend

Educators and ethicists (professionals who specialize in ethics-related issues) are distressed by how widespread cheating is today—and how its prevalence has steadily risen over the years. In 1957, for instance, University of Pennsylvania social sciences professor David E. Jacob surveyed a group of college students. He was shocked to find that at least 40 percent of the young people had frequently cheated, "often with no apology or sense of wrong-doing." Upon completion of the survey, Jacob was quoted in a newspaper article saying that at many universities, "systemic cheating on examinations is the custom rather than the exception."[29] Yet as shocking as that revelation was to Jacob, the incidence of cheating he uncovered during his study was low compared to what it is today. Recent studies have found up to 80 percent of students admit to cheating at some point.

A noted researcher who studied cheating trends among teenagers was the late Fred Schab, who was an educational psychologist at the University of Georgia. During a study that spanned two decades, Schab conducted three surveys of high schoolers: the first in 1969 involving 1,629 students; the next in 1979 with 1,100 students; and the third and final survey in 1989 with 1,291 students. The study was composed of a specially designed questionnaire, dialogue, and group discussions. Students responded to a number of issues: the amount of cheating they believed was going on, who was most guilty of cheating, reasons for the cheating, and the classes where the most cheating was taking place. The students were also asked to comment on how cheaters should be punished, societal beliefs about dishonesty, and their own dishonest behaviors in school (if applicable).

Schab published his study in the winter 1991 issue of the psychology journal *Adolescence*. With his opening sentence, Schab laid the foundation for the study's sobering findings: Cheating among high school students was common, and it was growing more problematic as time went by. "Cheating in high school has become an accepted fact among today's students," Schab wrote, "who apparently find it easier to cheat their way through courses than to rely on virtues like conscientious studies and honor achievements."[30]

Cheating Rises, Concern Grows

Schab's study had revealed that over the twenty-year period, students grew increasingly tolerant and accepting of cheating—even sometimes viewing it as a necessity. Specifically, in 1969 just 20 percent of students surveyed believed that most of their peers were guilty of cheating; by 1989 that percentage had grown to nearly 30 percent. The number of teens who admitted to using a cheat sheet while taking a test doubled from 34 percent in 1969 to 68 percent in 1989. Among the students surveyed, 58 percent admitted to letting others copy their work in 1969, but by 1989 the number had soared to 98 percent. When expressing their beliefs about whether good students cheated, only 16.7 percent believed that was true in 1969, and by 1989 the number had risen to 25.4 percent. A troubling finding over the twenty years the study was conducted was a steady and significant decline in the number of students who agreed with the statement "Honesty is the best policy." Whereas 82.3 percent thought the statement was true in 1969, the number dropped to less than 59.9 percent in 1989. "This research," Schab wrote in his 1991 paper, "clearly exposes the illegitimate learning practices of our high school students, which, if allowed to continue, will seriously damage the ambitious plans for improving American high schools."[31]

> The cheating facts that were revealed in Schab's 1989 study were eye-opening when he and his colleagues finished compiling the results—but the worst was yet to come.

The cheating facts that were revealed in Schab's 1989 study were eye-opening when he and his colleagues finished compiling the results—but the worst was yet to come. In 1998 the Josephson Institute Center for Youth Ethics released one of its first reports about the ethics of American teenagers, and the findings were bleak. Founder and president Michael Josephson stated: "This report card shows that the hole in our moral ozone is getting bigger. In terms of honesty and integrity, things are going from very bad to worse."[32] Years later the institute continued to find a significant, alarming prevalence of cheating, along with growing apathy on the part of students. When its 2002 report revealed that 74 percent of students had cheated during an exam during the previous year, Josephson issued a blunt warning about the climbing incidence of cheating:

> The evidence is that a willingness to cheat has become the norm and that parents, teachers, coaches, and even religious educators have not been able to stem the tide. The scary thing is that so many kids are entering the workforce to become corporate executives, politicians, airplane mechanics, and nuclear inspectors with the dispositions and skills of cheaters and thieves.[33]

A Positive Sign?

As bleak as things seemed in 2002, a report issued two years later indicated that the cheating situation among high schoolers was starting to show improvement. The number of teens who admitted to cheating on an exam dropped from 74 percent in 2002 to 62 percent in 2004. The number declined a little more by 2006, with 60 percent of students saying they had cheated on an exam. Two years later there was an inexplicable increase, jumping up to 64 percent of teens. But then there was another decline, which continued through 2010 and 2012.

> In November 2012, when the Josephson Institute issued its latest report, the results were more favorable than they had ever been.

In November 2012, when the Josephson Institute issued its latest report, the results were more favorable than they had ever been. Whereas the 2010 report had shown that 59 percent of students had cheated on an exam the prior year, the 2012 report revealed a drop to 51 percent. Education officials were not thrilled to see that more than half of the teens surveyed had cheated on tests, but they were pleased to see that cheating among young people might finally be declining. "It's a small ray of sunshine shining through lots of dark clouds," says Josephson. "Changes in children's behavior of this magnitude suggest a major shift in parenting and school involvement in issues of honesty and character. . . . Though there is still far too much cheating, lying and stealing, I think we have turned the corner."[34]

A Daunting Dilemma

Few experts would disagree that academic cheating is a serious, widespread problem across the United States. From the 1950s to the early 2000s, the incidence of cheating steadily rose. Also, surveys showed that it was becoming increasingly acceptable to students, which was deeply troubling to educators and ethicists. Then a 2012 report from the Josephson Institute of Ethics brought a glimmer of hope by showing a drop in the number of teens who had cheated the previous year. The institute, along with scores of individuals, hope that this is a sign of a more ethical future.

How Widespread Is Cheating Among Teens?

"Academic dishonesty is nothing new. As long as there have been homework assignments and tests, there have been cheaters."

—Matthew Lynch, "Cheating and Technology—Unethical Indifference," *Education Futures* (blog), *Education Week*, February 5, 2014. http://blogs.edweek.org.

Lynch is dean of the School of Education, Psychology, and Interdisciplinary Studies and an associate professor of education at Virginia Union University.

"Cheating rates have risen, and continue to be high."

—Eric M. Anderman, in NBC News Inside *Dateline*, "Why Do Kids Cheat? Facts About Cheating," April 29, 2012. http://insidedateline.nbcnews.com.

Anderman is director of Ohio State University's School of Educational Policy and Leadership and a professor of educational psychology.

* Editor's Note: While the definition of a primary source can be narrowly or broadly defined, for the purposes of Compact Research, a primary source consists of: 1) results of original research presented by an organization or researcher; 2) eyewitness accounts of events, personal experience, or work experience; 3) first-person editorials offering pundits' opinions; 4) government officials presenting political plans and/or policies; 5) representatives of organizations presenting testimony or policy.

66 At Harvard University, some 70 cheaters were booted for cheating on a government course exam despite it being open book, open notes and open Internet. 99

—Colman McCarthy, "Cheaters Justify Gaming the School System," *National Catholic Reporter*, December 19, 2013. http://ncronline.org.

McCarthy, a former *Washington Post* columnist, is now an educator who directs the Center for Teaching Peace in Washington, DC.

66 Because athletes must maintain a minimum grade-point average (GPA) to stay on the team and because they face great pressure related to their use of time, cheating is rampant among these students. 99

—Kevin Ryan and James Cooper, *Those Who Can, Teach*. Belmont, CA: Wadsworth, 2013, p. 118.

Ryan is professor emeritus of education at Boston University School of Education, and Cooper is professor emeritus at the University of Virginia's Curry School of Education.

66 Many people are surprised to hear just how prevalent cheating is among high school students. 99

—Challenge Success, "Cheat or Be Cheated? What We Know About Academic Integrity in Middle & High Schools & What We Can Do About It," 2012. www.challengesuccess.org.

Founded by three Stanford University psychologists, Challenge Success is an organization that works with schools and families to improve student well-being and engagement with learning.

66 Most college-bound students are exposed to significant cheating cultures during their high school years. 99

—Donald L. McCabe, Kenneth D. Butterfield, and Linda K. Treviño, *Cheating in College: Why Students Do It and What Educators Can Do About It*. Baltimore, MD: Johns Hopkins University Press, 2012, p. 6.

McCabe is a retired Rutgers University professor and a well-known authority on ethics and academic cheating; Butterfield is an associate professor of management, information systems, and entrepreneurship at Washington State University; and Treviño is a professor of organizational behavior at Pennsylvania State University.

❝Cheating has become the method of survival, the only way to reach and maintain the top for many . . . but there are better routes to reach number one while keeping your integrity intact.❞

—Sargunjot Kaur, "Academic Pressure," Palo Alto Medical Foundation, October 2013. www.pamf.org.

Kaur wrote this article as a journalism student at Mission San Jose High School in Fremont, California.

❝Data suggest that cheating too often is the rule, not the exception.❞

—Thomas Ehrlich and Ernestine Fu, "Cheating in Schools and Colleges: What to Do About It," *Forbes*, August 22, 2013. www.forbes.com.

Ehrlich, a professor at Stanford University's Graduate School of Education, and Fu, a Stanford PhD student, often collaborate to write about public service and social entrepreneurship.

❝As most of the studies on cheating rely on student self-reporting, cheating statistics depend on students' and researchers shared understanding of the definition of cheating, and that's a high hurdle to clear.❞

—Jessica Lahey, "A Classroom Where No One Cheats," *Atlantic*, December 2012. www.theatlantic.com.

Lahey is an English, Latin, and writing teacher from New Hampshire, as well as an author and contributing writer for the *New York Times* and the *Atlantic*.

How Widespread Is Cheating Among Teens?

- According to a 2012 survey by the Josephson Institute of Ethics, a decrease in student academic cheating occurred for the first time in a decade; in 2010, **59 percent** of students admitted to cheating on a test, and in 2012 this rate dropped to **51 percent**.

- In a June 2014 poll by a Detroit, Michigan, news website, people were asked whether they had ever cheated in school; **68 percent** said yes and **32 percent** said no.

- The Educational Testing Service reports that more than **75 percent** of college students admit to cheating in high school.

- According to a 2012 survey on academic integrity conducted at the University of Waterloo in Ontario, Canada, the most common form of academic misconduct is working with others when asked for individual work, which **32 percent** of undergraduate students report doing.

- The Educational Testing Service reports that **two-thirds** of middle school students have cheated on a test, and **nine-tenths** have copied another student's homework.

- According to a 2013 survey of freshmen at Harvard University, **10 percent** had cheated on an exam before college, and **42 percent** had cheated on a homework assignment.

Most Teens Admit to Cheating

One comprehensive study that confirmed the widespread prevalence of cheating was published in November 2012 by the Josephson Institute Center for Youth Ethics, which issues reports every other year on the ethics of American high school students. As this graph shows, more than 50 percent of teen participants admitted to cheating on a test at school and an even higher number said they had copied someone's homework.

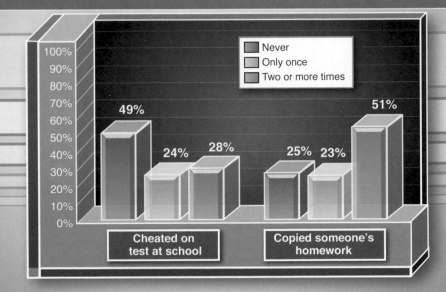

Source: Josephson Institute Center for Youth Ethics, *2012 Report Card on the Ethics of American Youth.* Los Angeles, CA: Josephson Institute of Ethics, November 2012. http://charactercounts.org.

- At Harvard University in the spring of 2012, **125 undergraduate students** were caught collaborating and plagiarizing a take-home final exam.

- According to a 2013 survey of freshmen at Harvard University, **20 percent** of athletes and **9 percent** of nonathletes admitted to cheating on an exam.

- According to a 2012 survey of Texas Tech University students, the majority of students understand what does and does not constitute cheating; however, nearly **30 percent** do not believe that collaborating without permission is cheating.

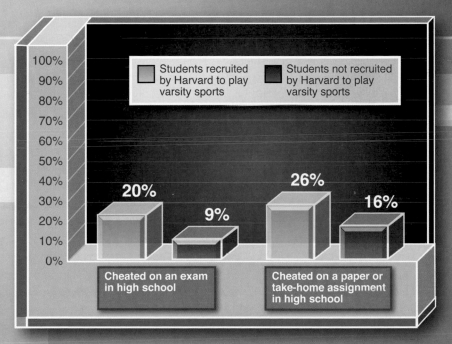

Harvard Students and Cheating

In 2013 Harvard University's student newspaper, the *Harvard Crimson*, surveyed incoming freshmen on the topic of cheating. Ten percent of respondents admitted to cheating on a high school exam, and 42 percent admitted to cheating on a homework assignment before coming to Harvard. As this graph shows, the survey also found that cheating among recruited athletes was higher than among students who were not recruited to play sports.

Students recruited by Harvard to play varsity sports

Students not recruited by Harvard to play varsity sports

100%
90%
80%
70%
60%
50%
40%
30%
20%
10%
0%

20%

9%

26%

16%

Cheated on an exam in high school

Cheated on a paper or take-home assignment in high school

Source: Madeline R. Conway and Cordelia F. Mendez, "Freshman Survey Part III: Classes, Clubs, and Concussions," *Harvard Crimson*, September 5, 2013. www.thecrimson.com.

- According to the International Center for Academic Integrity, **35 percent** of college officials and **41 percent** of the general public believe that academic cheating is a problem.

- A 2013 *Denver Post* article states that **60.8 percent** of students admitted to cheating, and of those, **16.5 percent** did not regret it.

- According to a 2013 survey of freshmen at Harvard University, men were twice as likely as women to cheat on a test and one and a half times as likely to cheat on a paper.

Setting the Record Straight About Cheating

According to the Stanford University–affiliated group Challenge Success, misconceptions about cheating are as widespread as cheating itself. Shown here are five of the most common misconceptions the group has identified.

Common Misconception	Fact
Cheating is not a problem at my kid's school.	Several studies indicate that between 80 and 95 percent of high school students admit to engaging in some form of cheating.
Kids cheat in the same ways today as they always have.	Cheating has evolved beyond cheat sheets (also called crib sheets) and wandering eyes to include plagiarizing from websites and "term-paper mills," using smartphones to look up answers during a test, and giving/receiving information about an exam through texting or sending pictures.
Only kids who struggle in school cheat.	Although cheating is common among low-achieving students, studies have found that it is also very common among high-achieving students.
Students who cheat do not think of it as wrong.	Surveys have revealed that many students who admit to cheating also admit to knowing it is wrong.
Cheating is unpredictable.	Research suggests that students cheat more when they believe grades and performance are valued in their classrooms, and they cheat less when they believe learning and subject mastery are valued.

Source: Challenge Success, "Cheat or Be Cheated? What We Know About Academic Integrity in Middle & High Schools & What We Can Do About It," 2012. www.challengesuccess.org.

- In July 2010 the *New York Times* reported that a male student at the University of Central Florida was caught trying to cheat on an exam by writing notes on his arm and incorporating them into his tattoos.

- According to the International Center for Academic Integrity, **86 percent** of high school students agree with the statement that most students cheat at some point.

How Has Technology Affected Teen Cheating?

> **Thanks to today's high-tech world, it's easier for kids to cheat—it just takes a few finger strokes of the keypad for someone to cut, paste and plagiarize.**
>
> —Laura Kastner, a clinical professor of psychiatry and psychology at the University of Washington and a psychologist in private practice who specializes in adolescent health.

> **Although we don't know whether technology has actually led to an increase in cheating, there is clear evidence that it has opened up new avenues for cheating.**
>
> —Challenge Success, an organization that works with schools and families to improve student well-being and engagement with learning.

In June 2014, when two teens crafted a plan to ace a final exam and help their classmates do the same, they forgot to consider one important detail: the teacher's close scrutiny of the test answers. At the time the two were juniors at Anderson High School, which is located in the Detroit, Michigan, suburb of Southgate. They timed their plan carefully; it took place between finals while teachers were in the hallway supervising students cleaning out their lockers. The coconspirators snuck into the classroom, found the answer key in the desk, and snapped pictures of it with their smartphones. Then they sent the photos in a group text to a number of other students, and the class convened to take the exam.

As is customary at Anderson High School, the teacher graded the exams right away and observed something that did not seem quite right. Out of thirty-plus students in the class, a suspiciously high number had achieved perfect scores.

Busted

The teacher immediately alerted administrators, and an investigation uncovered the cheating scheme. When confronted, the two students did not deny what they had done, although they told different versions of the story, as Southgate Community School District superintendent Leslie Hainrihar explains: "One maintains that they only used it for themselves, the other said that they took the picture and shared it with other students."[35] There was no way for staff to know exactly how many teens had used the answer key to cheat. Because of that, the entire class had to return to school during summer break and take the final exam over—but a different version this time.

> "Out of thirty-plus students in the class, a suspiciously high number had achieved perfect scores."

In a statement about the students who were behind the cheating incident, Hainrihar said that "consequences are forthcoming,"[36] but she would not elaborate. When asked whether all cell phones should be banned from school, she said that school officials were discussing that option and others. Hainrihar added that cheating is an age-old problem, not one created by technology. "Kids will try to cheat," she says. "We need to recognize what the temptations are and try to minimize them. The flip side is that there are many amazing instructional uses for the technology. Instead of banning them, can we use them . . . as an instructional tool? School districts will continue to look at it. It's an ongoing discussion."[37]

High-Tech Cheating

In one small, portable case, smartphones combine cellular phone technology with computing power, Internet access, and a digital camera that also shoots videos. These miniature supercomputers have revolutionized many aspects of people's lives. The popularity of smartphones is soaring, especially among young people, as a 2013 survey by the Pew Research Center Internet & American Life Project revealed. "Fully 95% of teens are online," says Pew, "a percentage that has been consistent since 2006. Yet, the nature of teens' internet use has transformed dramatically during that time—from stationary connections tied to desktops in the home to always-on connections that move with them throughout the day."[38]

In many ways, according to the March 2013 Pew report, teenagers represent the "leading edge in mobile connectivity." Research has shown that young people aged twelve to seventeen are just as likely to have a cell phone as they are to have a desktop computer or laptop. "And increasingly," the report states, "these phones are affording teens always-on, mobile access to the internet—in some cases, serving as their primary point of access. Smartphone ownership among teens has grown substantially since 2011." The Pew survey found that 23 percent of teens had a smartphone in 2011, and in just two years that number rose to 37 percent. In addition, close to one-fourth of teens own an iPad or other kind of tablet computer. "Taken together," the report authors write, "teens have more ways than ever to stay connected throughout the day—and night."[39]

> **Research has shown that young people aged twelve to seventeen are just as likely to have a cell phone as they are to have a desktop computer or laptop.**

As useful and indispensable (and fun) as smartphones can be, they have opened the door to a whole new realm of cheating opportunities. The Internet security firm Webroot explains:

> Most parents expect to hear cheating stories that include formulas written on wrists or knees, crib sheets hidden under a desk, or the infamous "flying V" (where students fan out diagonally from the person they intend to copy). But, it's essential parents begin including calculators, cell phones, and other connected technology devices (e.g. iPod Touch) in this list. More and more young people are using

these devices to cheat in school, and because this technology doesn't fall under traditional anti-cheating instruction, many students don't even consider it to be unethical.[40]

Webroot explains that common methods for smartphone cheating include storing notes on it (like a high-tech cheat sheet); sending text messages with questions, answers, or warnings about pop quizzes; looking up answers on the Internet; and taking pictures of a test for personal use and/or to share with classmates. In many cases, says Webroot, young people are not aware that they are doing anything wrong because "so many are immersed in the culture of free information available on the [Internet]."[41]

Social Media for Cheaters

In addition to all the smartphone-enabled cheating tactics described by Webroot, another example of high-tech cheating is teens who use their phones in conjunction with social media. For instance, they may take pictures of tests and/or answers, post them on social media sites such as Facebook and Instagram, and only let select people know about it. This took place at a number of California high schools on two different occasions: first in 2012 and again in 2013. Even though cell phones are prohibited at the schools during testing, teachers have a hard time preventing students from sneaking the phones in and using them secretively. This makes it difficult to keep cheating under control.

The first of these cheating incidents was discovered in April 2012, near the beginning of the state standardized testing period. An investigation revealed that one or more cell phones were used to take pictures of test questions, which were then posted online. A July 2012 *Los Angeles Times* article explains: "In all, 249 students posted 442 images on social-networking sites, including Facebook, Tumblr, Instagram, Webstagram and Pinterest. The 147 affected schools are spread across 94 school districts."[42]

A year later a similar incident happened in California, as well as on the other side of the country in New York. By the time the California scheme was discovered, students from 242 schools around the state had posted pictures to social media sites while taking standardized tests. Although most were just pictures of seemingly harmless items, such as the bubble art from answer sheets, students at sixteen of the schools posted actual test questions and answers. One student who was very upset about the incident was Ellisha Huntoon, who at the time was a junior at one of the sixteen schools. "It's a shock because our school is such a good school," she says. "You would never think the few kids would ever do something like that. But they did. I guess we have to suffer the consequences now."[43]

The New York incident, which also occurred in 2013, was in the town of West Islip, on Long Island. It involved a group of students who were using Facebook as a virtual gathering place to cheat on work for their biology class. School officials were alerted to the cheating scheme when the high school principal and the biology teacher both received an anonymous letter from a parent. According to Superintendent Richard Simon, a test answer sheet was photographed

> " School officials were alerted to the cheating scheme when the high school principal and the biology teacher both received an anonymous letter from a parent. "

and posted on Facebook while other students were still taking the test. "It started out as kids just trying to help each other," he says, "and it went beyond that."[44] After an investigation confirmed the cheating scheme, the Facebook page was taken down.

Gibberish for Sale

As indispensable as the Internet is for everything from communication and research to shopping and socializing, it has also opened up new avenues for unscrupulous tactics. One example is the paper mill (also called an essay mill), which is an online fulfillment service for written papers that people can obtain by paying a fee. Getting a paper from a paper mill is a blatant example of cheating (plagiarism) because someone is representing the work of another as his or her own.

Paper mills are flourishing, and an unfortunate number of people use their services. Yet Jonathan Bailey, creator and owner of a website that features plagiarism-related articles, emphasizes that this should not cause educators excessive worry. "Just because a method of plagiarism is on the rise doesn't mean that it's effective or that it can't be easily defeated," says Bailey. "Essay mills have a lot of problems that limit their usefulness as plagiarism tools and their impact on academics." Bailey goes on to say that in order to attract customers, essay mills must churn out work rapidly and cheaply, even while composing papers on highly specialized subjects. Says Bailey: "As Dan Ariely found when he purchased a series of essay mill papers for a survey, the papers themselves were almost gibberish in many cases and even showed heavy signs of plagiarism."[45]

Ariely is a professor of psychology and behavioral economics at Duke University. He worried about essay mills when he assigned his students papers to write. "The mills claim that the papers are meant to be used as reference material to help students write their own, original papers," says Ariely. "But with names such as echeat.com, it's pretty clear what their real purpose is." To find out for himself what essay mills were all about, and to see what sort of quality they provided, Ariely decided to place an order of his own. He selected four essay mills and provided each with criteria for a university-level term paper. "The topic of the paper?" he says. "Cheating."[46] Each of the mills that Ariely contacted accepted his request and quoted him between $150 and $216 to be paid in advance.

> " Paper mills are flourishing, and an unfortunate number of people use their services. "

When the essays arrived, Ariely says that to some degree they cured him of worrying about essay mills. "What we got back from the mills can best be described as gibberish," he says. There were "glaring errors" throughout the essays, sloppy and incomplete citations, and a writing quality that he describes as "awful." He shares a nonsensical paragraph contained in one of the papers: "'Cheating by healers. Healing is different. There is harmless healing, when healers-cheaters and wizards offer omens, lapels, damage to withdraw, the husband-wife back and stuff. We read in the newspaper and just smile. But these days fewer people believe in wizards."[47]

Ariely says the other papers were just as bad or worse, with two of them containing a large amount of plagiarized work. "It's comforting in a way that the technological revolution has not yet solved students' problems," he says. "They still have no other option but to actually work on their papers (or maybe cheat in the old-fashioned way and copy from friends). But I do worry about the existence of essay mills and the signal that they send to our students."[48]

Dishonesty Simplified

With each year, technology becomes more and more sophisticated and cheating becomes easier and easier. Smartphones, text messaging, and social media sites have enhanced opportunities and provided new methods for cheating. Rebecca Levey, cofounder of the video review site KidzVuz and a writer who specializes in technology and education, explains that most of the cheating taking place today is not actually new. Rather, she says, "it's a high tech version of what's always gone on. The difference is that it's much easier and the tools are readily available. The ways in which we now collaborate and share with ease online has made many facets of cheating seem like just an extension of this world."[49]

Primary Source Quotes*

How Has Technology Affected Teen Cheating?

66 Technology has increased the ways in which students can engage in cheating behaviors. 99

—Eric M. Anderman, in NBC News Inside *Dateline*, "Why Do Kids Cheat? Facts About Cheating," April 29, 2012. http://insidedateline.nbcnews.com.

Anderman is director of Ohio State University's School of Educational Policy and Leadership and a professor of educational psychology.

66 The real problem today with cheating is almost certainly concentrated in traditional classrooms, not online. 99

—Thomas K. Lindsay, "School for Scandal at Cheatin' U," *The Mark-Up* (blog), Real Clear Policy, September 17, 2014. www.realclearpolicy.com.

Lindsay is director of the Center for Higher Education at the Texas Public Policy Foundation.

* Editor's Note: While the definition of a primary source can be narrowly or broadly defined, for the purposes of Compact Research, a primary source consists of: 1) results of original research presented by an organization or researcher; 2) eyewitness accounts of events, personal experience, or work experience; 3) first-person editorials offering pundits' opinions; 4) government officials presenting political plans and/or policies; 5) representatives of organizations presenting testimony or policy.

Primary Source Quotes

"Today's students use smartphones, tablets or even in-class computers to aid their cheating endeavors and leave no trace of their crimes."

—Matthew Lynch, "Cheating and Technology—Unethical Indifference," *Education Futures* (blog), *Education Week*, February 5, 2014. http://blogs.edweek.org.

Lynch is dean of the School of Education, Psychology, and Interdisciplinary Studies and an associate professor of education at Virginia Union University.

"Technology is sometimes blamed for 'causing' academic dishonesty.... Students can easily use computers to plagiarize from Wikipedia or copy and paste from Google with just a few clicks."

—Berlin Fang, "Addressing Academic Dishonesty in the Age of Ubiquitous Technology," *Educause Review Online*, September 5, 2012. www.educause.edu.

Fang is director of instructional design at Abilene Christian University in Abilene, Texas.

"Computers can make cheating easier than ever before."

—David L. Jaffe, "Academic Cheating Fact Sheet," Perspectives in Assistive Technology, Stanford University, August 14, 2014. https://web.stanford.edu.

Jaffe is a class lecturer in Stanford University's Mechanical Engineering Department.

"We do not have good evidence to suggest that cheating is rampant in online courses—even though it is happening, and happening more than we would like, just like cheating in all of our courses."

—James M. Lang, *Cheating Lessons: Learning from Academic Dishonesty*. Cambridge, MA: Harvard University Press, 2013, p. 226.

Lang is an associate professor of English and director of the Center for Teaching Excellence at Assumption College in Worcester, Massachusetts.

66 **Right now . . . teachers and administrators around the nation refuse to face the facts that online cheating is a truly serious problem.** 99

—Michael Guista, "Online Cheating at American Colleges," *Lompoc (CA) Record*, November 3, 2013. http://lompocrecord.com.

Guista is a professor of English at Allan Hancock College in Santa Maria, California.

66 **Kids still cheat in familiar ways—copying from another kid's paper or sneaking in a cheat sheet on exam day—but students are also cheating in new ways, using technology to plagiarize essays or text test answers.** 99

—Denise Pope, "Academic Integrity: Cheat or Be Cheated?," *Edutopia* (blog), April 13, 2014. www.edutopia.org.

Pope is senior lecturer at Stanford University's Graduate School of Education and cofounder of the group Challenge Success, which works with schools and families to improve student well-being and engagement with learning.

How Has Technology Affected Teen Cheating?

- According to a 2013 *Denver Post* article, a popular paper mill website, School Sucks, receives abound **8,000 hits per day**.

- The plagiarism-detection service Turnitin reports that in 2012 the most commonly plagiarized site was Wikipedia, with Yahoo! Answers the second-most commonly plagiarized site.

- According to Jason Chu, senior education manager at Turnitin, many students have trouble synthesizing the wealth of information found online, so they wind up plagiarizing by copying whatever they find.

- Online security expert Robert Siciliano states that of **youth aged 10 to 20, 15 percent** have cheated on a test with a mobile device and **11 percent** have used a technique found online.

- According to the website Online-Education.net, **20 percent** of students search the Internet for answers to questions during a test.

- In a 2012 survey by OnlineCollege.org, **73 percent** of online students admitted to academic cheating.

- According to Plagiarism.org, **15 percent** of high school students admit they have obtained a paper from a term paper mill or website.

The Internet Makes Cheating Easier

Cheating by teens is nothing new, but the Internet presents opportunities that never before existed. For would-be cheaters, the ability to copy web pages, paste them into Word documents, and turn the papers in as their own work (known as plagiarism) has never been so easy. Whether teens have ever done this was one of the questions asked during 2012 study by the Josephson Institute Center for Youth Ethics. As shown here, at least 14 percent of all students admitted to copying from the Internet for an assignment, with older teens more likely to have done it two or more times.

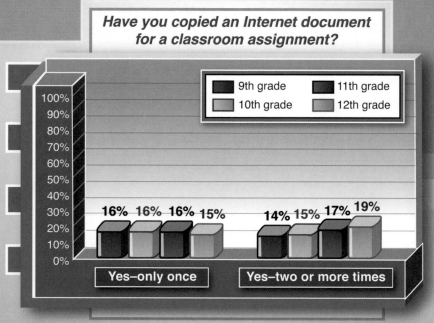

Have you copied an Internet document for a classroom assignment?

- 9th grade
- 10th grade
- 11th grade
- 12th grade

Yes—only once: 16% 16% 16% 15%

Yes—two or more times: 14% 15% 17% 19%

Source: Josephson Institute Center for Youth Ethics, *2012 Report Card on the Ethics of American Youth.* Los Angeles, CA: Josephson Institute of Ethics, November 2012. http://charactercounts.org.

- The website Online-Education.net states that **26 percent** of students store information on their phones to use during a test.

- According to the website Online-Education.net, **one-fourth** of students do not consider checking notes on a cell phone or the Internet to be cheating, nor do they consider texting friends test answers to be cheating.

High-Tech Plagiarism

Using or imitating someone else's work and passing it off as one's own is known as plagiarism, and its incidence has soared in the past few decades largely due to the Internet. In 2012 an Oakland, California, company that specializes in plagiarism prevention technology released a listing of ten categories that it collectively refers to as the "plagiarism spectrum." The spectrum is shown here in order of most to least problematic in academic settings.

	Clone	The act of submitting another's work, word for word, as one's own.
	CTRL-C	A written piece that contains significant portions of text from a single source without alterations.
	Find-Replace	Changing key words and phrases but retaining the essential content of the source in a paper.
	Remix	Paraphrasing from other sources and making the content fit together seamlessly.
	Recycle	Borrowing generously from one's own previous work without citation (self-plagiarize).
	Hybrid	Combining perfectly cited sources with copied passages, without citation, in one paper.
	Mashup	A paper that represents a mix of copied material from several different sources without proper citation.
	404 Error	A written piece that includes citations to nonexistent or inaccurate information about sources.
	Aggregator	This paper includes proper citation but almost no original work.
	Re-tweet	Includes proper citation but relies too closely on the text's original wording and/or structure.

Source: Turnitin, "The Plagiarism Spectrum: Tagging 10 Types of Unoriginal Work," May 2012. www.turnitin.com.

- In a 2012 survey on academic integrity conducted at the University of Waterloo in Ontario, Canada, **12 percent** of undergraduate respondents indicated that on more than one occasion, they had copied information from an electronic source without citing it.

- According to Turnitin, two of the most common methods of cheating are copying large portions of a text found online and mixing copied material from multiple online sources; more than **8 in 10 cheaters** have used these methods.

- Online security expert Robert Siciliano says that **60 percent** of college students and **49 percent** of teens have looked up an answer during a test or for an assignment online.

Why Do Teens Cheat?

> **"**Cheating is associated with certain characteristics: impulsivity, low levels of academic confidence, and attending a school where the belief is that 'everyone cheats.'**"**
>
> —Eric M. Anderman, director of Ohio State University's School of Educational Policy and Leadership and a professor of educational psychology.

> **"**If my teaching practices create an atmosphere in which students resort to cheating rather than rely on their own hard work and discovery, I'm doing something wrong.**"**
>
> —Jessica Lahey, an English, Latin, and writing teacher from New Hampshire who is also an author and contributing writer for the *New York Times* and the *Atlantic*.

In December 2013 former *Washington Post* columnist Colman McCarthy published an article about a study that he conducted with his high school and college students. Now an educator who serves as director of the Center for Teaching Peace in Washington, DC, McCarthy asked the students to answer one question: "If you have a chance to cheat on an exam and with no risk at all of getting caught, what's your choice?"[50] McCarthy instructed the young people to write their answers down and hand them in, and he assured them that whatever they said would remain completely anonymous.

After he had collected all the papers, McCarthy tabulated the results—and was taken aback to find that 80 percent of his students were willing to cheat. Further review of their papers showed that the would-be cheaters fell into one of two categories. "The first group justified gaming the system because they felt the system was already gaming them," says McCarthy, who goes on to describe the second group as the "out-and-out opportunists."[51]

To Cheat or Not to Cheat

Among the first group, or those who McCarthy says felt justified in bending the rules (gaming the system) because the system was gaming them, the responses were indicative of the students' disdain for the education system's testing and grading policies. A common objection was the extraordinarily heavy focus on grades, with one student saying that grades are all that matter and it should not be that way. Another bluntly stated: "Yes I would cheat. The entire grading system is centered on judging students based on how they take tests. It's not fair. If the system wants you to get a good grade, the pressure of college, GPA and a career will cause students to crack, to cheat."[52]

One of McCarthy's students said that he would cheat because a good grade is all that matters and that most things taught in school are not useful in real life anyway. Another acknowledged that cheating may not be the right thing to do, but there did not seem to be much choice. "Yes I would cheat," the student wrote. "I know it's wrong but I've been taught and raised in a result-based society. If I didn't feel so pressured to do well in school I probably wouldn't."[53]

> "One of McCarthy's students said that he would cheat because a good grade is all that matters and that most things taught in school are not useful in real life anyway."

McCarthy refers to the second group as "opportunists" because their justification for cheating revolved around their own personal gain, and *opportunism* means taking advantage of situations for selfish reasons. As with the first group, these students were also focused on grades. One high schooler admittedly would cheat to secure the types of grades that colleges would want and expect, and another student would cheat, if it became necessary, in order to get high enough grades to graduate. A third student in this group saw no problem whatsoever with cheating if that was what it took to be successful. "I would cheat because why not?" the student wrote. "It hurts nobody and the only outcome is a better grade for myself, which boosts my chances for a better future."[54]

Among the 20 percent of students in McCarthy's study who said they would not cheat under any circumstances, their answers were closely aligned with their personal values and how they would feel if they cheated. One of them spoke of not being able to cheat because of the inevitable guilt; another mentioned the paranoia that would result from cheating, and a third spoke of having a strong conscience derived from years of attending Catholic school. One of the students was especially blunt about the importance of honesty, writing: "Frankly I don't think I would cheat. Cheating brings stress and fear and just makes you feel like a total piece of crap. There is no sense of pride when you do well on a test you've cheated on."[55]

> " Although teens who cheat may feel justified in doing so, the fact is that cheating is a form of unethical behavior. "

Growing Apathy About Ethics

Although teens who cheat may feel justified in doing so, the fact is that cheating is a form of unethical behavior. Experts warn that those who regularly engage in cheating may eventually become jaded about the importance of ethics. Over time, personal integrity may become less and less of a priority, crowded out by the resolve to do whatever it takes to succeed. "When students cheat," says the NYU Child Study Center, "their sense of right and wrong changes. In other words, the more one cheats, the easier it becomes to rationalize one's behavior and cheat again."[56]

Michael Josephson, president of the Josephson Institute of Ethics, says that repeated cheating "creates its own gravitational force." He explains: "The very act of cheating and getting away with it significantly increases the chances you'll do it again." Josephson says that he finds it distressing to see such erosion of ethics in society. "Cheating is wrong—unequivocally wrong—and it undermines social institutions and personal integrity." Yet Josephson goes on to say that the situation is not all gloom and doom. "We haven't lost our moral compass. People, including kids, still have a pretty good notion of right and wrong, though there is a great tendency to rationalize."[57]

In December 2013 Jessica Lahey, who is an English, Latin, and writing teacher from New Hampshire, was shocked by a letter she received from a college student. He had read an article Lahey published in which she theorized that widespread cheating was, to a large degree, the result of classroom culture. She assumed that her readers (as well as her students) understood that cheating was wrong, but the letter she received made her realize she was mistaken. The student who sent it to Lahey started out with a blunt statement, saying, unapologetically, "I cheated all throughout high school." He went on to cite all his achievements while in school, including National Merit Scholar, editor in chief of the school newspaper, and valedictorian of his class. "To most educators," he wrote, "my true story is a disgrace to the system."[58] From reading his letter, it was clear to Lahey that the young man had no problem with cheating.

The letter writer went on to explain why he felt perfectly justified in cheating his way through high school. Referring to what he had done as "principled cheating," he rationalized that cheating was necessary in the classes where he felt he was being cheated out of a good education. Lahey explains: "He'd responded by cheating right back in retaliation." Being faced with the student's confession and subsequent justification of his dishonesty was upsetting for Lahey. "It's one thing to read the statistics on cheating," she says, "but it was quite another to be faced [with] a real-life example of a student cheater."[59]

Blurred Lines

Today's teens have never known a time without the Internet. They have become accustomed to finding answers to everything they need with a few clicks of a mouse or a series of taps on a smartphone or tablet. They are used to sharing: cutting and pasting in e-mails, exchanging photos with friends, and sharing the latest happenings on social media sites. So it can be confusing when young people are told that some types of information sharing are unacceptable. "I definitely think there's a mindset problem," says Carol Baker, curriculum director for science and music at a school near Chicago, Illinois. "Today, kids are used to obtaining any kind of information they want (online). There are so many things that are free out there. I think kids don't have the same sense of, 'Gee, it's wrong to take something that somebody else wrote.' The Internet encourages all of us to do that."[60]

This sort of confusion was evident in a letter received by education writer and former teacher Leanna Landsmann. It was from a woman whose seventh-grade daughter had received a zero on a report and had absolutely no idea why. The mother said this happened "'because her teacher says almost all of it was stolen from the Internet.'" The girl had told her mother that "everyone does it" and she did not understand why it was considered cheating. To Landsmann, the mother wrote: "Don't schools teach students research skills?"[61]

> **One high-profile cheating scandal involving a famous sports figure was that of former world champion cyclist Lance Armstrong.**

Landsmann replied that yes, schools do teach proper research and writing techniques to students. But she also acknowledged the difference between using material from the Internet for research and copying it verbatim, which is clearly an act of plagiarism. "Teens are so used to sharing information online," says Landsmann, "that many don't understand that they can't just grab a photo, poem or paragraph, and then weave it into an assignment and pass the work off as their own."[62]

Societal Influence

Just by virtue of their age (and associated hormonal changes), teens tend to be impressionable. For instance, peer pressure can be a powerful influence on teens, which is why so many become involved with drugs and alcohol, as well as exhibit impulsive behaviors and poor decision making. Teens can also be influenced by people whom they admire and look up to. If someone they consider an idol is caught cheating, young people may instinctively feel defensive of the person. In the process, they may develop the impression that cheating is acceptable because highly successful people do it.

One high-profile cheating scandal involving a famous sports figure was that of former world champion cyclist Lance Armstrong. After winning the world-famous Tour de France cycling race seven times, Armstrong was charged with having used illegal performance-enhancing drugs. Although he initially denied using the substances, the evidence against him was incriminating, and he was stripped of his seven titles. In addition, he received a lifetime ban on competing in cycling or any other sports that follow the World Anti-Doping Agency Code. In an October 2012 report, the US Anti-Doping Agency referred to the Armstrong cheating scandal as "the most sophisticated, professionalized and successful doping program that sport has ever seen."[63] The following year, Armstrong publicly acknowledged that he had used performance-enhancing drugs throughout his cycling career.

> "Because teen cheating has become so widespread, examining the causes is a priority for researchers who study adolescent behavior."

Young people's exposure to such highly publicized dishonesty was discussed in a September 2012 article by Erika Christakis, an early childhood educator at the Yale University Child Study Center, and Nicholas A. Christakis, codirector of Yale's Institute for Network Science. In the article, they draw a connection between the dishonesty that teens observe every day and the high incidence of cheating. "Nowadays, we seem to live in a culture of lies," they write. "Should we really be surprised that high schoolers cheat on standardized tests when they grow up among adults—Olympic cyclists, politicians, money managers, high school administrators, journalists, professors and even their own parents—who may be thrifty, at best, with the truth?"[64]

Gaming and Cheating

Because teen cheating has become so widespread, examining the causes is a priority for researchers who study adolescent behavior. In November 2013 a team of researchers from the United States, Italy, and Netherlands announced the findings of a study that examined the connection between violent video games and dishonest conduct among teens. It involved 172 Italian high school students who were randomly assigned to one of two groups: one that played a violent video game (such as *Grand Theft Auto*) and another that played a nonviolent game.

After playing their assigned games for thirty-five minutes, the teens were asked to solve a ten-item logic test. The researchers explained that for each answer teens got correct, they would be rewarded with a raffle ticket that they could exchange for a prize, such as an iPad. After the researchers had graded the tests, they told each teen how many questions he or she had answered correctly. Then, based on an honor system, the teens were told to take the proper number of raffle tickets from an envelope: one for each correct answer. They were not aware that the researchers knew how many tickets were in each envelope, which allowed them to determine whether participants took more than they had earned. At the conclusion of the study, the researchers found that teens who played violent video games were at least eight times more likely to cheat than those who played nonviolent games. Says Brad Bushman, Ohio State University professor of education and psychology and coauthor of the study: "We have consistently found in a number of studies that those who play violent games act more aggressively, and this is just more evidence."[65]

A Complex Problem

Why teens cheat is not an easy question to answer. Innumerable factors come into play, from a lack of clear understanding of what constitutes cheating to diminishing ethics, the pressure to succeed, and societal influence. Additional answers may be discovered in the future as research on the hows and whys of cheating continues.

Primary Source Quotes*

Why Do Teens Cheat?

Primary Source Quotes

66 Students cheat because they are morally bankrupt or because they are responding inappropriately to a context [educators] have structured for them. 99

—James M. Lang, *Cheating Lessons: Learning from Academic Dishonesty*. Cambridge, MA: Harvard University Press, 2013, p. 220.

Lang is an associate professor of English and director of the Center for Teaching Excellence at Assumption College in Worcester, Massachusetts.

66 Though students typically know that what they're doing is wrong, they justify their actions by saying that they just 'didn't have a choice—it's cheat or be cheated.' They feel enormous pressure to get the grades and test scores they believe they'll need for future success. 99

—Denise Pope, "Academic Integrity: Cheat or Be Cheated?," *Edutopia* (blog), April 13, 2014. www.edutopia.org.

Pope is senior lecturer at Stanford University's Graduate School of Education and cofounder of the group Challenge Success, which works with schools and families to improve student well-being and engagement with learning.

* Editor's Note: While the definition of a primary source can be narrowly or broadly defined, for the purposes of Compact Research, a primary source consists of: 1) results of original research presented by an organization or researcher; 2) eyewitness accounts of events, personal experience, or work experience; 3) first-person editorials offering pundits' opinions; 4) government officials presenting political plans and/or policies; 5) representatives of organizations presenting testimony or policy.

66 The issue of cheating is fundamentally one of character. 99

—Thomas Ehrlich and Ernestine Fu, "Cheating in Schools and Colleges: What to Do About It," *Forbes*, August 22, 2013. www.forbes.com.

Ehrlich, a professor at Stanford University's Graduate School of Education, and Fu, a Stanford PhD student, often collaborate to write about public service and social entrepreneurship.

66 Just as an honor code can promote ethical attitudes and behavior, a strong peer cheating culture can have the opposite effect. 99

—Donald L. McCabe, Kenneth D. Butterfield, and Linda K. Treviño, *Cheating in College: Why Students Do It and What Educators Can Do About It*. Baltimore, MD: Johns Hopkins University Press, 2012, p. 6.

McCabe is a retired Rutgers University professor and a well-known authority on ethics and academic cheating; Butterfield is an associate professor of management, information systems, and entrepreneurship at Washington State University; and Treviño is a professor of organizational behavior at Pennsylvania State University.

66 Cheating no longer carries the stigma that it used to. Less social disapproval coupled with increased competition for admission into universities and graduate schools has made students more willing to do whatever it takes to get the A. 99

—David L. Jaffe, "Academic Cheating Fact Sheet," Perspectives in Assistive Technology, Stanford University, August 14, 2014. https://web.stanford.edu.

Jaffe is a class lecturer in Stanford University's Mechanical Engineering Department.

❝Students' feelings about themselves matter. When students feel concerned about their academic capabilities or expect poor outcomes, they are more likely to cheat.❞

—Challenge Success, "Cheat or Be Cheated? What We Know About Academic Integrity in Middle & High Schools & What We Can Do About It," 2012. www.challengesuccess.org.

Founded by three Stanford University psychologists, Challenge Success is an organization that works with schools and families to improve student well-being and engagement with learning.

❝Since cheating through technology is not listed specifically as being against the rules in many school policies, students do not view the actions as unethical.❞

—Matthew Lynch, "Cheating and Technology—Unethical Indifference," *Education Futures* (blog), *Education Week*, February 5, 2014. http://blogs.edweek.org.

Lynch is dean of the School of Education, Psychology, and Interdisciplinary Studies and an associate professor of education at Virginia Union University.

❝Middle school students cheat more than elementary students because of increased pressures to get high grades."

—Laura Kastner, "Your Cheatin' Teen: How to Deal When Kids Cheat," *Parent Map*, August 29, 2013. www.parentmap.com.

Kastner is a clinical professor of psychiatry and psychology at the University of Washington and a psychologist in private practice who specializes in adolescent health.

Facts and Illustrations

Why Do Teens Cheat?

- **Forty-five percent** of boys and **29 percent** of girls surveyed in 2012 by the Josephson Institute of Ethics believe that it is acceptable for people to occasionally lie and cheat.

- According to the Educational Testing Service, one likely catalyst for academic cheating is the increased competition for admission into universities.

- A 2012 academic integrity survey conducted at the University of Waterloo in Ontario, Canada, found that students view cheating as far less serious than faculty members do.

- A 2013 *Denver Post* article reports that the average GPA of students who admitted to cheating was **3.41**, whereas the average GPA of students who did not cheat was **2.85**.

- Research published in 2012 by the American Psychological Association states that people who cheat rank high in certain personality types, including narcissism and psychopathy.

- In 2012 Harvard University professor Howard Gardner told the *New York Times* that one motivation behind academic cheating is the desire of many students to keep up with other students who they believe are also cheating.

Many Theories About Why

Even though teens who cheat have their own personal reasons for doing so, experts have identified some shared traits. Shown here are some of the most common reasons for student cheating, according to the mental health and research organization New York University Child Study Center.

Why Students Cheat

Pressure	Increasing pressure to succeed academically, combined with technology that is widely available and provides an easy means of cheating (such as smartphones), have contributed to a culture of cheating across many schools.
Motivation	Students who are solely motivated by getting ahead rather than by the learning process itself are at higher risk of cheating.
Ethical Standards	When students cheat, their sense of right and wrong changes; in other words, the more one cheats, the easier it becomes to rationalize one's behavior and cheat again.
Peer Behavior	If students see others cheating and getting away with it, they are more likely to cheat themselves in order to stay competitive.
Perceptions of Teachers	Students are more likely to cheat if they see a teacher as unfair and uncaring and focused solely on grades.
Perceptions of Schoolwork	If students see classes and assignments as arbitrary, it is easier to justify cheating.
Grade-Focused Environment	Classes in which there is an emphasis on extrinsic goals (such as good grades) instead of mastery goals (learning and improvement) have been linked to cheating.

Source: New York University Child Study Center, "Cheating in School: Why It Happens and How to Prevent It," October 2012. www.aboutourkids.org.

Associating Cheating with Success

As part of its 2012 survey involving more than twenty-three thousand American high school students, the Josephson Institute of Ethics presented teens with statements about cheating and asked whether they agreed or disagreed. As shown here, teenage boys were more likely than girls to agree that cheating was closely linked to success.

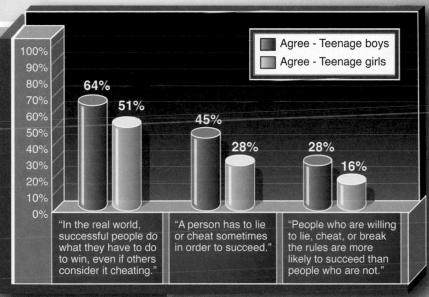

Teenagers who agree with statements about ethics—boys versus girls

- Agree - Teenage boys
- Agree - Teenage girls

Statement	Boys	Girls
"In the real world, successful people do what they have to do to win, even if others consider it cheating."	64%	51%
"A person has to lie or cheat sometimes in order to succeed."	45%	28%
"People who are willing to lie, cheat, or break the rules are more likely to succeed than people who are not."	28%	16%

Source: Josephson Institute Center for Youth Ethics, *2012 Report Card on the Ethics of American Youth*. Los Angeles, CA: Josephson Institute of Ethics, November 2012. http://charactercounts.org.

- According to a 2012 survey by the Josephson Institute of Ethics, **1 in 5 boys** and **1 in 10 girls** believe that an act does not count as cheating if the majority of their peers are also doing it.

- Point Loma Nazarene University says one reason students cheat is that an illness or a job may have hampered their preparation for an exam.

Blame It on the Brain

For years scientists have known that adolescents' brains are not fully developed, and that the last part to develop (in someone's early twenties) is the prefrontal cortex. This section, which is located at the front of the brain behind the forehead, is responsible for such tasks as regulating behavior, impulse control, choosing between right and wrong, and decision making. A widely accepted scientific theory is that the underdeveloped adolescent brain is at least partly responsible for bad choices like using drugs or alcohol, deciding to smoke, risk taking, and cheating. This illustration shows the location of the prefrontal cortex at the front of the brain.

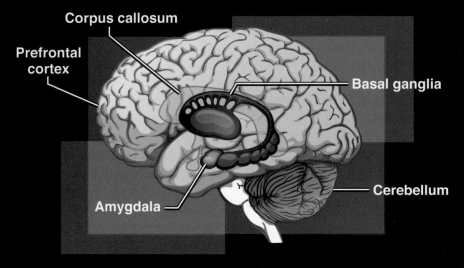

Source: A. Rae Simpson, "Brain Changes." MIT Young Adult Development Project. http://hrweb.mit.edu.

- Eric M. Anderman, chair of Ohio State University's Department of Educational Studies, says that the pressure to get high grades is one motivator for cheating; students who feel their school places a higher value on academic performance than on learning are more likely to cheat.

- According to Point Loma Nazarene University, a common cause of cheating is simply a student seizing an opportunity; for instance, the instructor leaving the room or another student not covering his or her paper.

How Should Teen Cheating Be Addressed?

66Everyone at the institution—from the president of the university and the board of directors right on down to every janitor and cafeteria worker—has to buy into the fact that the school is an academically honest institution and that cheating is a reprehensible behavior.99

—Stephen F. Davis, emeritus professor of psychology at Emporia State University in Emporia, Kansas, and coauthor of the book *Cheating in School: What We Know and What We Can Do*.

66Instead of viewing the entire student body as potential cheaters, institutions should create a supportive environment in which students can learn through positive reinforcements.99

—Berlin Fang, director of instructional design at Abilene Christian University in Abilene, Texas.

Although there are many possible solutions for addressing academic cheating, putting a stop to it is far from easy for educators. "Eradicating cheating from a classroom is a remarkably difficult task," says Jessica Lahey, a teacher who is also an author and contributing writer for the *New York Times* and *Atlantic* magazine. She goes on to say that today's educators struggle to keep up with students' "novel and ingenious" methods of academic dishonesty, "and yet we forever remain one step behind our technologically and ethically flexible wards." Another by-product of cheating, according to Lahey, is that when it is widespread teachers inevitably start to doubt themselves. "Cheating taps into teachers' worst fears about both our ability to teach and our trust in our students," she says. "I never doubt my perceptions more than when I contemplate whether to confront a student about suspicions of cheating. No matter how the process shakes out, trust is broken, feelings are hurt, and everyone loses sleep."[66]

Anti-Cheating Efforts

Although many schools have cheating policies in place, researchers who specialize in academic cheating say that enforcement of these policies is often lax. One example is Stuyvesant High School, where rules are often enforced based on the individual situation, rather than strictly adhering to policy. Students have said in interviews that teachers sometimes bend rules, or overlook them completely, to avoid the student being unduly harmed. After catching someone cheating on a test, for instance, some teachers allow him or her to retake the test rather than adhering to policy-driven punishments ranging from an automatic zero to suspension.

In a December 2012 *New York Times* article, journalist Vivian Yee describes one incident at Stuyvesant that she learned about through an interview: "A recent graduate said that near the end of her senior year, a teacher caught one of the student's friends taking a math test with a sheet of formulas held in her lap. But knowing that the girl had been accepted into an Ivy League school, the teacher let the student off with a warning because he did not want to jeopardize her enrollment."[67]

As awareness grows of widespread student cheating, schools across the country are reviewing their cheating policies to make them more effective. At Palo Alto High School, administrators determined that their policy was too harsh and focused too heavily on punishment. Under the policy, for instance, a student receives an automatic zero for the first assignment he or she cheats on, and the teacher is required to notify administration about the incident. If the student is caught cheating a second time, in any class, he or she is dropped from the class and receives an automatic F. A third cheating incident results in these same consequences, along with a five-day suspension. According to Palo Alto High School teacher Grant Blackburn, actual punishment under this stringent policy is rare, and only a fraction of students who cheat are ever reported to administrators.

In crafting their new policy, administrators involved students in the process. The end result was a policy that emphasizes education and information more than punishment. The hope is that a less punitive policy will motivate teachers to report cheating incidents, while at the same time providing students with an opportunity to change their behavior. Susan Bailey, who worked on the policy development committee, says that student improvement should be the ultimate objective of the high school's cheating policy. "Honesty should be emphasized at school," she says, "but in high school you have to have the opportunity to make mistakes and learn from them."[68]

Face It, Deal with It

With studies showing disturbing numbers of teens cheating throughout the United States, many ethics professionals say that finding ways to effectively curb cheating should be a higher priority. The lack of urgency is troubling to Richard Jarc, who is executive director of the Josephson Institute: "No one seems to be saying, 'Oh my god, we have to do something about it,'" he says. "It's pretty scary. These kids are going to school to become doctors, lawyers, and bridge builders. I don't want one of them to be my bridge builder or my doctor."[69]

Denise Pope, who is a senior lecturer at Stanford University's Graduate School of Education and cofounder of the Stanford-affiliated group Challenge Success, also believes in the importance of anti-cheating efforts. In December 2012 Pope was interviewed by the educational publication *NEA Today*, and she discussed a number of issues related to academic cheating, such as how widespread it is, the role of technology in cheating, and which teens are most likely to cheat, among other topics. When asked what can be done to curtail cheating, Pope emphasized the importance of bringing it out in the open. "Cheating is a taboo subject— many schools just don't want to talk about it,"[70] she says.

Pope goes on to explain that denial plays a huge role in a school's willingness to address a cheating problem and implement programs to curb cheating. If this does not happen, she says, cheating will continue and undoubtedly become an even bigger problem. Pope explains:

> One of the big misconceptions is that "That's not a problem at our school!" when in fact it occurs everywhere.

And people think if they don't talk about it, then it won't happen. But admitting cheating exists in your schools is a big first step. . . . If you talk about it, admit there's a problem, come up with a way to show it won't be tolerated, and have everyone sign onto doing something about it, cheating can be curbed.[71]

Building a Culture of Honesty

Because technology has blurred the lines between what is acceptable and what crosses the line into cheating, experts are convinced that there needs to be a greater focus on ethics; in other words, teens need to be reminded of the reasons why ethical behavior is so important. Stanford University public service and philanthropy experts Thomas Ehrlich and Ernestine Fu state that cheating is fundamentally an issue of character. "Character is most readily molded during times of transition, and adolescence is prime among them," they write. "High school and college are, therefore, particularly important places for students to learn that when they cheat in their academic work, they are not only cheating fellow students and their institution; they are cheating themselves."[72]

> "Because technology has blurred the lines between what is acceptable and what crosses the line into cheating, experts are convinced that there needs to be a greater focus on ethics."

It is widely accepted among experts that frequent reinforcement of honesty and integrity can go a long way toward preventing cheating. But research has shown that most schools neglect to make this a priority. Josephson Institute of Ethics president Michael Josephson says that few schools "place any meaningful emphasis on integrity, academic or otherwise, and colleges are even more indifferent than high schools. When you start giving take-home exams and telling kids not to talk about it, or you let them carry smartphones into tests, it's an invitation to cheating."[73]

Student-Led Effort

According to cognitive psychologist David A. Rettinger, getting students involved in creating a culture of academic honesty can be very effective in curbing cheating. "The key," he says, "is to create this community feeling of disgust at the cheating behavior. And the best way to do that is at the student level."[74] This was the philosophy behind the formation of a group at the University of California–San Diego (UCSD) called Academic Integrity Matters (AIM). AIM's focus is to raise awareness about the problem of cheating in schools, as well as educate college students, high school students, parents, and educators about the importance of—and benefits of—academic integrity.

Because it is important for students to understand what is and is not appropriate and to be aware of UCSD's strong commitment to integrity and ethics, all freshmen are required to complete an online tutorial on academic integrity. This must be completed before they can register for their second-semester classes. An American Psychological Association article explains: "Professors are also encouraged to explain the importance of academic integrity in their syllabi and to take time during the first week of class to talk about the behaviors that constitute cheating in their courses, as well as the consequences for engaging in those behaviors."[75]

> "According to cognitive psychologist David A. Rettinger, getting students involved in creating a culture of academic honesty can be very effective in curbing cheating."

One of AIM's activities has entailed circulating a student petition that urges faculty members to provide more education on academic integrity. Also requested in the petition is for faculty to more explicitly state the rules for academic integrity in the classroom and to be vigilant about reporting all cheating whenever they become aware of it. The idea for a petition came from an AIM survey that asked UCSD professors for their opinions on the current state of academic integrity at UCSD. Nick Graham, the UCSD student who led the development of the petition, explains: "One of the conclusions we reached from this survey was that professors think students don't care about the promotion of integrity at UCSD. We saw that as a huge problem and so we developed the petition. The signatures we have accrued so far are a testament to the fact that students want UCSD to be a place of integrity and that they both need and want professors' help."[76]

Should Smartphones Be Banned?

When people become aware of how prolific cheating is among teens, and that smartphones are often used to accomplish that cheating, many express disbelief that these gadgets are even allowed in the classroom at all. People often view the banning of smartphones as one of the most sensible, uncomplicated solutions to curbing academic cheating. Douglas M. Winneg, who is founder and CEO of the Newton Upper Falls, Massachusetts, firm Software Secure, refers to today's smartphone as "the lock-pick of cheating."[77] Winneg emphasizes how easy cheating can be with these high-tech devices. They can store entire databases of test questions and answers, allow students to text back and forth to exchange information during class, and connect to Wikipedia and other online resources. At the very least, Winneg argues, schools should consider collecting smartphones at the classroom door on test days.

> "People often view the banning of smartphones as one of the most sensible, uncomplicated solutions to curbing academic cheating."

Although schools throughout the United States have enacted policies that restrict the use of smartphones, not all students abide by the rules. This was true during the 2012 cheating scandal at Stuyvesant High School in New York City. The proctor (a teacher's designate who supervises the test taking) did not see that the ringleader of the incident, Nayeem Ahsan, was using his iPhone. As someone who had cheated repeatedly, Ahsan had become very clever about keeping the phone concealed with his elbow bent around it. "The problem is that phones are very small," says tech security expert Larry Magid. "People have them in their pocket and it's very easy to pull one out, take a picture, put it away. It's a good possibility you'd get away with it."[78]

While many people agree that smartphones must be restricted in classrooms, not everyone believes that banning them is the answer. This is the perspective of Sarah Togo, a parent from Palo Alto Hills, California. Togo says that her family used to live in a community where cheating with smartphones was rampant at the high school. But she is convinced that banning them will not stop cheating, as she explains:

> This is a high-pressure school, like Stuyvesant, and there are always more cheating issues at such schools, public or private. In the local case, though, the pressure was from the parents far, far more than from the high school itself. Cell phones were just an easy, discreet enabler. Take them away and these over-pressured kids will find another way.[79]

Looking Ahead

As promising as many strategies can be for curtailing cheating among teens, experts stress that this will be no easy task. "Cheating is a many-headed hydra," says Lahey. "Cut one offense off, and another one bursts forth in its place."[80] Experts say that one of the highest priorities in the battle against cheating is to educate young people on the importance of integrity and honesty. In time, this could help them learn to care more about how well they do in school—for the right reasons. Also, teens need to fully understand their boundaries, such as the difference between using the Internet for research and pla-

> " As promising as many strategies can be for curtailing cheating among teens, experts stress that this will be no easy task.

giarizing. Another strategy that may help prevent or curb cheating is focusing more on learning and less on grades. By having a greater focus on these and other techniques, educators may be able to eventually succeed in bringing cheating under control.

Primary Source Quotes*

How Should Teen Cheating Be Addressed?

❝For the same reason that we think it sensible for police cars to have distinctive markings that are visible on highways—as a deterrent to speeders—we believe that deterrents to cheating should be put in place by teachers.❞

—Thomas Ehrlich and Ernestine Fu, "Cheating in Schools and Colleges: What to Do About It," *Forbes*, August 22, 2013. www.forbes.com.

Ehrlich, a professor at Stanford University's Graduate School of Education, and Fu, a Stanford PhD student, often collaborate to write about public service and social entrepreneurship.

....

❝My concern with a heavy deterrence focus is that some students may feel that if they can avoid getting caught, then there is nothing more to think about.❞

—Alan Reifman, "Academic Dishonesty: Prevalent but Preventable," *On the Campus* (blog), *Psychology Today*, February 1, 2012. www.psychologytoday.com.

Reifman is a professor of human development and family studies at Texas Tech University.

....

* Editor's Note: While the definition of a primary source can be narrowly or broadly defined, for the purposes of Compact Research, a primary source consists of: 1) results of original research presented by an organization or researcher; 2) eyewitness accounts of events, personal experience, or work experience; 3) first-person editorials offering pundits' opinions; 4) government officials presenting political plans and/or policies; 5) representatives of organizations presenting testimony or policy.

"We'll always have some small degree of cheating; that's just human. But the best defense we have against cheating is excellence in course design and teaching.**"**

—James M. Lang, "Why the Hottest Trend in Online Education Already Has a Cheating Problem," Daily Dot, September 9, 2013. www.dailydot.com.

Lang is an associate professor of English and director of the Center for Teaching Excellence at Assumption College in Worcester, Massachusetts.

"An increasing number of colleges and universities are refocusing their efforts to promote academic integrity among students, as part of their strategy to enhance students' ethical development and reduce the level of cheating on campus.**"**

—Donald L. McCabe, Kenneth D. Butterfield, and Linda K. Treviño, *Cheating in College: Why Students Do It and What Educators Can Do About It.* Baltimore, MD: Johns Hopkins University Press, 2012, p. 11.

McCabe is a retired Rutgers University professor and a well-known authority on ethics and academic cheating; Butterfield is an associate professor of management, information systems, and entrepreneurship at Washington State University; and Treviño is a professor of organizational behavior at Pennsylvania State University.

"From our own work with schools and our white paper reviewing 15 years of research on academic integrity, we have found that schools can use a number of effective strategies to reduce cheating rates.**"**

—Denise Pope, "Academic Integrity: Cheat or Be Cheated?," *Edutopia* (blog), April 13, 2014. www.edutopia.org.

Pope is senior lecturer at Stanford University's Graduate School of Education and cofounder of the group Challenge Success, which works with schools and families to improve student well-being and engagement with learning.

"In order to earn our place at the front of a cheating-free classroom, educators are going to have to own our share of the blame for the atmosphere of high-stakes testing and extrinsic rewards that we've created.**"**

—Jessica Lahey, "A Classroom Where No One Cheats," *Atlantic*, December 2012. www.theatlantic.com.

Lahey is an English, Latin, and writing teacher from New Hampshire, as well as an author and contributing writer for the *New York Times* and the *Atlantic*.

66 Honor codes have been shown to reduce cheating, and are most effective when students are required to sign honor code pledges immediately before tests. 99

—NYU Child Study Center, "Cheating in School: Why It Happens and How to Prevent It," October 2012. www.aboutourkids.org.

The NYU Child Study Center seeks to improve the treatment of child psychiatric disorders through scientific practice, research, and education.

66 Given the high rates of cheating across many groups and settings, and the various rationales that students use for their cheating behavior, it may seem impossible to promote a climate of academic integrity in K–12 schools. 99

—Challenge Success, "Cheat or Be Cheated? What We Know About Academic Integrity in Middle & High Schools & What We Can Do About It," 2012. www.challengesuccess.org.

Founded by three Stanford University psychologists, Challenge Success is an organization that works with schools and families to improve student well-being and engagement with learning.

66 What can parents do? They need to take a strong stand—and make it clear to their teens that representing work taken from another source as their own is cheating. 99

—Laura Kastner, "Your Cheatin' Teen: How to Deal When Kids Cheat," *Parent Map*, August 29, 2013. www.parentmap.com.

Kastner is a clinical professor of psychiatry and psychology at the University of Washington and a psychologist in private practice who specializes in adolescent health.

Facts and Illustrations

How Should Teen Cheating Be Addressed?

- According to a 2012 survey on academic integrity conducted at the University of Waterloo in Ontario, Canada, many students and faculty members believe that unique assignments and easier reporting of academic misconduct would lower academic cheating rates.

- Challenge Success, an organization affiliated with Stanford University, states that parents who offer external rewards such as money for good grades diminish the goal of learning over success, which fosters cheating.

- Online security expert Robert Siciliano suggests that parents talk with their children about their online activity and set limits on smartphone and tablet usage, especially in the classroom, in order to curb academic cheating.

- The University of Central Florida's testing center has taken numerous measures to curb student cheating, one of which is installation of an overhead camera to capture suspicious activity during test taking.

- OnlineCollege.org urges professors to stop using multiple-choice tests and to use assignments that make cheating difficult, such as essay exams and term papers.

Students Favor Expulsion for Cheaters

In a 2012 survey of Texas Tech students, the university's Ethics Center asked students for their opinions on the appropriate punishment for academic dishonesty. A large number of the 484 students who answered this question said they favored expulsion, followed by failing the test, assignment, and/or class.

"In the past, students have said that Texas Tech should have more severe consequences for academic dishonesty. If you agree, what specific consequences would you suggest?"

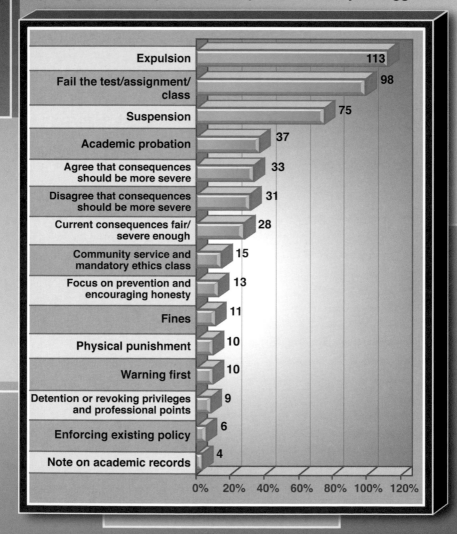

Response	Value
Expulsion	113
Fail the test/assignment/class	98
Suspension	75
Academic probation	37
Agree that consequences should be more severe	33
Disagree that consequences should be more severe	31
Current consequences fair/severe enough	28
Community service and mandatory ethics class	15
Focus on prevention and encouraging honesty	13
Fines	11
Physical punishment	10
Warning first	10
Detention or revoking privileges and professional points	9
Enforcing existing policy	6
Note on academic records	4

Note: Students were allowed to give more than one response.

Source: Texas Tech University Ethics Center, *Arbor Day Academic Integrity Survey Report*, June 2012. www.depts.ttu.edu.

Cheating Prevention Strategies

Ethics specialists and educators acknowledge that cheating may never be completely eradicated, but there are a number of steps schools can take to curb the practice. The strategies shown here are recommended by a March 2014 article in the publication *Education Week*.

• Collect cell phones from students before testing begins to thwart photographs being taken of tests or questions, to prevent texting others for answers, and to block access to the Internet.
• If a test is given online, make sure students are using a secure browser that prevents them from surfing the Internet or accessing apps.
• Consider hiring a company that monitors social-networking sites such as Instagram or Twitter during testing windows to determine whether test questions or photos of exams have been posted.
• Use adaptive tests. Some experts say that because adaptive testing means each student's exam is likely to be different, this method makes it much more difficult to cheat.
• If using online tests in which students all get the same questions, consider placing cloth, plastic, or cardboard barriers between computer monitors so students cannot see each other's screens.
• Provide in-depth training for proctors and do spot checks to make sure they are adhering to protocol.

Source: Michelle R. Davis, "Adaptive Tech., Secure Browsers Aim to Curb Student Cheating," *Education Week*, March 13, 2014.

- Some professors, such as economics professor Ray Fair of Yale University, address cheating by encouraging students to work together so long as each final product is individual and all collaborators are credited.

- Challenge Success, an organization affiliated with Stanford University, urges parents to foster academic integrity by talking with their children about academics in a way that emphasizes learning instead of grades.

One School's Approach to Addressing Cheating

High schools throughout the United States have policies and procedures in place to deal with students who are caught cheating. Shown here is the Academic Honesty Policy for Troy High School in Fullerton, California, where school officials treat cheating as a serious offense.

The Student . . .

- Will receive an automatic zero (failing grade) on the assignment or test; no make-up work will be offered to compensate for the zero.

- Will be dropped from the class with no credit if the student is involved in an act of academic dishonesty in the class where he or she is a student aide.

- Will serve a four-hour Saturday School. The student will receive a "U" (unsatisfactory) in citizenship on the semester grade report.

- Will be dropped from the National Honor Society (NHS) if the student is a member of that organization.

- Will be dropped from the California Scholarship Federation (CSF) if the student is a member of that organization.

- May face suspension from extracurricular activities, including sports programs.

- May face suspension from Troy High School.

- May face expulsion from the Fullerton Joint Union High School District.

- May be removed from the course with a grade of "F" (failure).

Source: Troy High School, "Troy High School Academic Honesty Policy," 2014. www.troyhigh.com.

- New anti-cheating measures instituted at the University of Central Florida's testing center have lowered the cheating rate to a mere **14 suspected incidents** out of **64,000 tests** administered.

- According to a 2012 survey of Texas Tech University students, **50 percent** would be interested in taking a plagiarism education workshop.

- Challenge Success, an organization affiliated with Stanford University, suggests that to reduce cheating, teachers should emphasize learning over grades and get to know their students as individuals.

Key People and Advocacy Groups

Eric M. Anderman: Chair of the Department of Educational Studies at Ohio State University. He has published dozens of articles on educational psychology, with a focus on adolescents and their behavior. Anderman is also coauthor of the books *Classroom Motivation* and *Psychology of Academic Cheating*.

Asia Pacific Forum on Educational Integrity: A nonprofit organization based in Australia that fosters research and collaboration on issues related to academic integrity, including ethical research and writing practices. It sponsors conferences, a discussion forum, and a newsletter, all focusing on topics related to educational integrity.

Character Education Partnership: A Washington, DC–based nonprofit organization that works with schools to help teach students ethical values such as honesty, fairness, and responsibility. Its members train educators on ways to build character in students, using its 11 Principles of Effective Character Education program, which outlines aspects of character education such as providing students with opportunities for moral action.

Josh Corngold: An associate professor of education at the University of Tulsa. He studies ethical and philosophical issues in education and is an authority on the issue of academic cheating in high school and college. Corngold is the coauthor of *Educating for Democracy: Preparing Undergraduates for Responsible Political Engagement*.

Thomas Ehrlich and Ernestine Fu: Writers and contributors to *Forbes* and coauthors of the book *Civic Work, Life Lessons*. Ehrlich has worked in the US government and high positions of leadership in multiple universities. Fu has started numerous projects and organizations to promote youth leadership and service. They commonly work together in public service and have published articles about a variety of topics, including cheating in school.

Tricia Gallant: Author of *Academic Integrity in the Twenty-First Century* and coauthor of *Cheating in School: What We Know and What We Can Do*. Gallant is an authority on the topic of educational ethics and serves on the Advisory Council of the International Center for Academic Integrity.

International Association of Academic Integrity Conferences: An alliance of experts on academic integrity and plagiarism from the United States, United Kingdom, and Australia that works to raise awareness on academic cheating and encourage international discussion. It also supports research initiatives on how to properly address the current rise in cheating among students.

International Center for Academic Integrity: An association of more than two hundred learning institutions that work to combat cheating, plagiarism, and academic dishonesty and to promote a culture of academic honesty among students and teachers around the world. The center holds an annual conference on topics related to academic integrity.

Josephson Institute Center for Youth Ethics: A nonprofit organization that seeks to uphold ethical behavior in multiple fields, including education, law enforcement, journalism, and the military. It conducts a survey every two years on the ethics of American high school students.

James M. Lang: An associate professor of English and director of the Center for Teaching Excellence at Assumption College in Worcester, Massachusetts. Lang has written several books on education, including *Cheating Lessons: Learning from Academic Dishonesty*, as well as a monthly column on teaching and learning for the *Chronicle of Higher Education*.

Donald L. McCabe: An authority on academic cheating and the founder of the International Center for Academic Integrity, which works to combat academic cheating, plagiarism, and academic dishonesty. McCabe has surveyed tens of thousands of college and high school students about cheating.

National Center for Fair & Open Testing: Also known as FairTest, a nonprofit group that advocates equal opportunity and fairness in academic testing. In a 2013 press release, FairTest revealed widespread corruption related to standardized test scores across the nation. The organization publishes an electronic newsletter, the *Examiner*, as well as several fact sheets related to testing in public schools and universities.

David A. Rettinger: An associate professor of psychology at the University of Mary Washington in Fredericksburg, Virginia. He has conducted extensive research and published articles in several journals on the subject of academic integrity.

Robert Siciliano: An author and an online security expert with computer security firm McAfee. He maintains a blog in which he explores technology-related topics, including high-tech cheating in schools.

Dave Tomar: A graduate of Rutgers University and a freelance writer. Using the pseudonym "Ed Dante," he wrote an article in the *Chronicle of Higher Education* in which he confessed to writing term papers—including doctoral dissertations—for other students. He later published *The Shadow Scholar*, a book describing his lucrative business as a ghost writer for custom essays. His confessions helped provide a deeper view of academic cheating and how often it occurs.

Adam Wheeler: A former Harvard student who forged his résumé, application, and other documents to be accepted into the school. During his third year Harvard discovered that some of Wheeler's award-winning work had been plagiarized, and he was expelled. His fraudulent educational career is documented in the book *Conning Harvard: Adam Wheeler, the Con Artist Who Faked His Way into the Ivy League*.

Chronology

1601
In his play *Poetaster*, English author Ben Jonson becomes the first person to use the term *plagiary* (from the Latin for "kidnapper") in print to describe a literary thief.

1941
An article in the *Journal of Higher Education* cites a dramatically higher incidence of cheating among members of college fraternities; this is attributed to the requirement that members maintain a high grade point average.

1997
Plagiarism detection service Turnitin is launched by iParadigms, a company that was founded by graduate student researchers at the University of California–Berkeley to monitor the reuse of academic papers.

1966
A study published in the journal *Social Problems* reports that as many as 49 percent of college students are guilty of cheating.

1600 1940 1960 1980

1938
A survey published in the *School Board Journal* finds that the majority of students who admit to academic cheating justified their cheating on the grounds that it was necessary in order to keep up with other students who cheated.

1965
The *New York Times* publishes an article titled "Survey Reveals Cheating on Rise in New York City's High Schools," in which high school honor students admit to cheating on exams by writing notes on rubber bands, their fingernails, the palms of their hands, shirt cuffs, and ties.

1992
The Center for Academic Integrity, today known as the International Center for Academic Integrity, is founded in Maryland.

1964
Columbia University researcher William J. Bowers publishes a landmark study titled *Student Dishonesty and Its Control in College*; it reveals that deans and student body presidents of accredited US colleges rank academic dishonesty second among student discipline problems.

1989
The journal *Adolescence* reports that almost 30 percent of surveyed students believe that the majority of their peers cheat in school—whereas only 20 percent believed so in 1969.

1990
A survey at Miami University finds that 91 percent of all college students admit they have cheated in school.

2000
In its annual survey of high school students, *Who's Who Among American High School Students* finds that 80 percent of high-achieving teens admit to some form of academic dishonesty.

2012
A cheating scandal at New York City's prestigious Stuyvesant High School results in one student being expelled, dozens of others being suspended, and significant changes in administration.

2014
Eleven students are expelled from Corona del Mar High School in Orange County, California, for their involvement in a cheating scandal, which entailed hacking into school computers, altering grades, and stealing exams.

2007
The first iPhone is released; its easy access to web resources and social networks leads some experts to speculate that it may spark further academic cheating in the classroom.

2010
The *New York Times* reports that in surveys of fourteen thousand college students over the previous four years, an average of 61 percent admitted to cheating on assignments and tests.

2000

2010

2001
Researcher Donald L. McCabe surveys forty-five hundred high school students and reports that 74 percent admit to cheating on a test one or more times.

2012
The *Los Angeles Times* reports that thirty-six questions from standardized exams in schools throughout California have shown up on social media sites.

2008
Two separate cheating incidents at Chapel Hill High School in North Carolina lead to the suspension of four students: two who used a camera phone to copy an exam, and two others who broke into a teacher's office and stole an AP history exam.

2011
Twenty people are arrested in an SAT cheating scandal on Long Island in New York, in which high school students were accused of paying others up to $2,500 to take the test for them.

2009
A national poll finds that more than 35 percent of teens admitted to cheating via cell phones and the Internet, including texting answers to each another during tests, storing notes and information on their smartphones, and downloading research papers to turn in as their own work.

Related Organizations

Academic Integrity Matters (AIM)
301 University Center
University of California–San Diego
La Jolla, CA 92093
phone: (858) 822-2163 • fax: (858) 534-7925
e-mail: aic@ucsd.edu • website: http://ucsdaim.org

AIM is a nonprofit organization that works to educate students, parents, schools, and teachers about the problem of cheating in schools and the importance of academic integrity. Its website offers information about upcoming events, guidelines for the AIM Contest, a newsletter, videos, and more.

Asia Pacific Forum on Educational Integrity (APFEI)
University of South Australia
101 Currie St.
Adelaide, SA 5001, Australia
phone: +61 8 8302 6611
e-mail: contact@apfei.edu.au • website: http://apfei.edu.au

The APFEI is a nonprofit organization based in Australia that fosters research and collaboration on issues related to academic integrity, including ethical research and writing practices. Its website contains news, information on upcoming conferences and events, a discussion forum, case studies, a newsletter, research papers, and a link to the twice-yearly *International Journal for Educational Integrity*.

Character Education Partnership (CEP)
1634 I St. NW, Suite 550
Washington, DC 20006
phone: (202) 296-7743
website: www.character.org

The CEP is a Washington, DC–based nonprofit organization that works with schools to help teach students ethical values such as honesty and responsibility. Its website offers webinars, a webstore, a calendar of upcoming events, and information on its 11 Principles of Effective Character Education program, which outlines aspects of character education such as providing students with opportunities for moral action. The CEP publishes the *Journal of Research in Character Education*, which focuses on helping young people develop core ethical values such as fairness and respect for self and others.

International Association of Academic Integrity Conferences (IAAIC)

website: www.iaaic.org

The IAAIC is an alliance of experts on academic integrity and plagiarism, with members from the United States, United Kingdom, and Australia. It works to raise awareness on academic cheating and plagiarism and to encourage international discussion on these issues. It also supports research initiatives on how to properly address the current rise in cheating among students. The IAAIC website has news, information on upcoming events, and numerous links to publications and other organizations related to academic integrity and plagiarism.

International Center for Academic Integrity (ICAI)

126 Hardin Hall
Clemson University
Clemson, SC 29634-5138
phone: (864) 656-1293 • fax: (864) 656-2858
e-mail: CAI-L@clemson.edu • website: www.academicintegrity.org

The ICAI is an association of 360 high schools, colleges, and universities that work to combat cheating, plagiarism, and academic dishonesty. Its website offers information about upcoming events and projects such as the Character Counts! program, news, research, and resources such as its *Fundamental Values of Academic Integrity* booklet.

Josephson Institute of Ethics

9841 Airport Blvd., #300
Los Angeles, CA 90045
phone: (310) 846-4800; toll-free: (800) 711-2670 • fax: (310) 846-4858
website: http://josephsoninstitute.org

The Josephson Institute is a nonprofit organization that seeks to uphold ethical behavior in multiple fields, including education, law enforcement, journalism, and the military. Its website contains information on character-building programs, a blog, videos, brochures, a newsletter, and an online store.

National Center for Fair & Open Testing

PO Box 300204
Jamaica Plain, MA 02130
phone: (617) 477-9792
website: www.fairtest.org

Also known as FairTest, this nonprofit group advocates equal opportunity and fairness in academic testing. In a 2013 press release, FairTest revealed widespread corruption related to standardized test scores across the nation. The organization publishes an electronic newsletter, the *Examiner*, as well as several fact sheets related to testing in public schools and universities.

Plagiarism Advice

6–8 Charlotte Square
Newcastle upon Tyne NE1 4XF
phone: +44 (0)191 2111 986 • fax: +44 (0) 845 643 9015
e-mail: plagiarismadvice@iparadigms.com
website: www.plagiarismadvice.org

Plagiarism Advice was formed in 2002 to raise awareness of plagiarism and academic dishonesty in learning institutions around the world. Its website offers resources such as webinars, information on plagiarism detection software, information on conferences, and links to outside resources such as a plagiarism discussion forum and a plagiarism blog.

Transparency International

1023 Fifteenth St. NW, Suite 300
Washington, DC 20005
phone: (202) 589-1616 • fax: (202) 589-1512
e-mail: transparency@transparency-usa.org
website: www.transparency.org

This organization monitors and publicizes international corporate and political corruption. Its website includes the 2013 policy brief titled "Preventing Undue Influence and Preserving Academic Integrity," which outlines steps to help prevent plagiarism and other forms of academic dishonesty.

21st Century Information Fluency Project (21CIF)
PO Box 1091
Warrenville, IL 60555
e-mail: help@21cif.com • website: http://21cif.com

The 21CIF provides resources to help teachers and students find, evaluate, and use online information in an effective and ethical manner. Its website includes a Citation Wizard tool to help students cite sources properly and avoid inadvertent plagiarism.

For Further Research

Books
Thomas Ehrlich and Ernestine Fu, *Civic Work, Civic Lessons: Two Generations Reflect on Public Service*. Lanham, MD: University Press of America, 2013.

Peggy M. Houghton and Timothy J. Houghton, *Plagiarism: Suicide for Grades*. Flint, MI: Baker College, 2014. Kindle edition.

James M. Lang, *Cheating Lessons: Learning from Academic Dishonesty*. Cambridge, MA: Harvard University Press, 2013.

Hal Marcovitz, *Teens & Cheating*. Philadelphia, PA: Mason Crest, 2014.

Donald L. McCabe, Kenneth D. Butterfield, and Linda K. Treviño. *Cheating in College: Why Students Do It and What Educators Can Do About It*. Baltimore, MD: Johns Hopkins University Press, 2012.

Dave Tomar, *The Shadow Scholar: How I Made a Living Helping College Kids Cheat*. New York: Bloomsbury USA, 2012.

Christian Wayne, *Academic Dishonesty: When Students Cheat and Plagiarize*. Upper Darby, PA: Solstice Media, 2012. Kindle edition.

Julie Zauzmer and Xi Yu, *Conning Harvard: Adam Wheeler, the Con Artist Who Faked His Way into the Ivy League*. New York: Globe Pequot, 2012.

Periodicals
Eliza Anyangwe, "Academic Integrity 2.0: Maintaining Values and Openness in a Digital World," *Guardian* (Manchester), July 6, 2012.

Rachel Aviv, "Wrong Answer," *New Yorker*, July 21, 2014.

Al Baker, "At Top School, Cheating Voids 70 Pupils' Tests," *New York Times*, July 9, 2012.

Thomas Ehrlich and Ernestine Fu, "Cheating in Schools and Colleges: What to Do About It," *Forbes*, August 22, 2013.

Lawrence Hardy, "An Epidemic of Cheating," *American School Board Journal*, July/August 2013.

Robert Kolker, "Cheating Upwards," *New York Magazine*, September 16, 2012.

Jessica Lahey, "A Classroom Where No One Cheats," *Atlantic*, December 12, 2013.

Jessica Lahey, "'I Cheated All Throughout High School,'" *Atlantic*, December 24, 2013.

James M. Lang, "How College Classes Encourage Cheating," *Boston Globe*, August 4, 2013.

Richard Pérez-Peña, "Studies Find More Students Cheating, with High Achievers No Exception," *New York Times*, September 7, 2012.

Rebecca D. Robbins, "Harvard Investigates 'Unprecedented' Academic Dishonesty Case," *Harvard Crimson*, August 30, 2012.

Sue Shellenbarger, "How Could a Sweet Third-Grader Just Cheat on That School Exam?," *Wall Street Journal*, May 15, 2013.

Natasha Velez, Georgett Roberts, and Jamie Schram, "Teen Student Jumps to Death After She's Caught Cheating," *New York Post*, May 30, 2014.

Tim Walker, "What Can Be Done About Student Cheating?," *NEA Today*, December 11, 2012.

Jeffrey R. Young, "Online Classes See Cheating Go High-Tech," *Chronicle of Higher Education*, June 3, 2012.

Internet Sources

Rich Jarc, "The Ethics of American Youth: 2012," Josephson Institute Center for Youth Ethics, November 20, 2012. http://charactercounts. org/programs/reportcard/2012/installment_report-card_honesty -integrity.html.

Bruce Johnson, "Is High Tech Cheating a Threat to Online Education?," Online College Courses, June 6, 2012. www.onlinecollege courses.com/2012/06/06/is-high-tech-cheating-a-threat-to-online -education.

Nannette Miranda, "STAR Test Cheating: Students Post Photos on Social Media," ABC30 Action News, August 9, 2013. http://abc30 .com/archive/9201918.

Julia Rubin, "Cheating Runs Rampant in Schools Across the Country—but Does It Pay Off?," *Huffington Post*, December 11, 2013. www.huffingtonpost.com/2013/12/11/cheating-runs-rampant-in -schools_n_4427216.html.

Kim Russell, "Nearly Entire Class Caught Cheating on Final Exam at Anderson High School in Southgate," WXYZ.com, June 17, 2014. www.wxyz.com/news/nearly-entire-class-caught-cheating-on-final -exam-at-anderson-high-school-in-southgate.

Kara Vincent, "Award-Winning Study Sheds Light on Academic Dishonesty in Canada," *YOURblog*, January 10, 2013. www2.uregina.ca /yourblog/award-winning-study-sheds-light-on-academic-dishon esty-in-canada.

Source Notes

Overview

1. Laura Kastner, "Your Cheatin' Teen: How to Deal When Kids Cheat," *Parent Map*, August 29, 2013. www.parentmap.com.
2. Robert Kolker, "Cheating Upwards," *New York Magazine*, September 16, 2012. http://nymag.com.
3. Kolker, "Cheating Upwards."
4. Quoted in Vivian Yee, "Stuyvesant Students Describe the How and the Why of Cheating," *New York Times*, September 25, 2012. www.nytimes.com.
5. KidsHealth, "Cheating," September 2013. http://kidshealth.org.
6. NYU Child Study Center, "Cheating in School: Why It Happens and How to Prevent It," October 2012. www.aboutourkids.org.
7. Quoted in Julie Shapiro, "Cheating Prevalent at High-Pressure Stuyvesant High School, Students Say," DNAinfo New York, June 29, 2012. www.dnainfo.com.
8. Denise Pope, interviewed by Tim Walker, "What Can Be Done About Student Cheating?," *NEA Today*, December 11, 2012. http://neatoday.org.
9. Josephson Institute of Ethics, "2012 Report Card on the Ethics of American Youth," November 2012. http://charactercounts.org.
10. Robert Siciliano, "Cheating and Bullying: It's a Bigger Problem than You Think!," McAfee, July 31, 2013. http://blogs.mcafee.com.
11. Quoted in John Keilman, "New Technology Lets Students Cheat More than Ever," *Business Insider*, August 7, 2012. www.businessinsider.com.
12. Quoted in Kellie B. Gormly, "Internet Creates a Rise in Cut-and-Paste Plagiarism," TribLive, January 23, 2012. http://triblive.com.
13. Quoted in Keilman, "New Technology Lets Students Cheat More than Ever."
14. Quoted in Sharon Noguchi, "Among Many Teens, Cheating Is Part of School," *San Jose (CA) Mercury News*, July 12, 2012. www.mercurynews.com.
15. Thomas Ehrlich and Ernestine Fu, "Cheating in Schools and Colleges: What to Do About It," *Forbes*, August 22, 2013. www.forbes.com.
16. Quoted in Amy Novotney, "Beat the Cheat," *Monitor on Psychology*, June 2011. www.apa.org.
17. Quoted in Noguchi, "Among Many Teens, Cheating Is Part of School."
18. Quoted in Noguchi, "Among Many Teens, Cheating Is Part of School."
19. NYU Child Study Center, "Cheating in School."
20. NYU Child Study Center, "Cheating in School."
21. Ehrlich and Fu, "Cheating in Schools and Colleges."
22. Challenge Success, "Cheat or Be Cheated? What We Know About Academic Integrity in Middle & High Schools & What We Can Do About It," 2012. www.challengesuccess.org.

How Widespread Is Cheating Among Teens?

23. Quoted in Emma Decker, "Cheater," *Grant Magazine* (Grant High School, Portland, OR), March 21, 2013. http://grantmagazine.com.
24. Quoted in Decker, "Cheater."
25. Quoted in Decker, "Cheater."

26. Quoted in Decker, "Cheater."
27. Hannah Fry and Joe Mozingo, "Corona del Mar High Students Expelled in Cheating Scandal," *Los Angeles Times*, January 29, 2014. http://articles.latimes.com.
28. Quoted in Fry and Mozingo, "Corona del Mar High Students Expelled in Cheating Scandal."
29. Quoted in *Wilmington (Ohio) News*, "Prof Says Students Cheat on Exams, Not with Love," March 5, 1957, p. 14.
30. Fred Schab, "Schooling Without Learning: Thirty Years of Cheating in High School," *Adolescence*, Winter 1991.
31. Schab, "Schooling Without Learning."
32. Michael Josephson, "Josephson Institute Report Card," Josephson Institute Center for Youth Ethics, 1998. http://charactercounts.org.
33. Michael Josephson, "Josephson Institute Report Card."
34. Quoted in Rich Jarc, "The Ethics of American Youth: 2012," November 20, 2012. http://charactercounts.org.

How Has Technology Affected Teen Cheating?

35. Quoted in CBS News, "Downriver High School Students Caught in Cheating Scandal After Entire Class Gets 100%," June 17, 2014. http://detroit.cbslocal.com.
36. Quoted in James Mitchell, "Students Share Stolen Answers, Retake Test," *Dearborn (MI) Times-Herald*, June 23, 2014. http://downriversundaytimes.com.
37. Quoted in Mitchell, "Students Share Stolen Answers, Retake Test."
38. Mary Madden, Amanda Lenhart, Maeve Duggan, Sandra Cortesi, and Urs Gasser, "Teens and Technology, 2013," Pew Research Center Internet & American Life Project, March 13, 2013. www.pewinternet.org.
39. Madden et al., "Teens and Technology, 2013."
40. Webroot, "Cheating and Technology: How Teens Do It." www.webroot.com.
41. Webroot, "Cheating and Technology."
42. Howard Blume, "Students' Online Photos of California Tests Delay Release of Scores," *Los Angeles Times*, July 18, 2012. http://articles.latimes.com.
43. Quoted in Nannette Miranda, "Star Test Cheating Students Post Photos on Social Media," ABC News, August 9, 2013. http://abc7.com.
44. Quoted in Candice Ferrett, "West Islip Superintendent: 12 Students Punished After Using Facebook to Cheat," *Newsday*, May 23, 2013. www.newsday.com.
45. Jonathan Bailey, "Are Essay Mills Worth Worrying About?," Plagiarism Today, February 9, 2012. www.plagiarismtoday.com.
46. Dan Ariely, "Essay Mills—a Coarse Lesson on Cheating," *Los Angeles Times*, June 17, 2012. http://articles.latimes.com.
47. Ariely, "Essay Mills—a Coarse Lesson on Cheating."
48. Ariely, "Essay Mills—a Coarse Lesson on Cheating."
49. Rebecca Levey, "5 Ways Students Use Technology to Cheat—What Parents Need to Know," Mashable, September 28, 2012. http://mashable.com.

Why Do Teens Cheat?

50. Colman McCarthy, "Cheaters Justify Gaming the School System," *National Catholic Reporter*, December 19, 2013. http://ncronline.org.
51. McCarthy, "Cheaters Justify Gaming the School System."
52. Quoted in McCarthy, "Cheaters Justify Gaming the School System."

53. Quoted in McCarthy, "Cheaters Justify Gaming the School System."
54. Quoted in McCarthy, "Cheaters Justify Gaming the School System."
55. Quoted in McCarthy, "Cheaters Justify Gaming the School System."
56. NYU Child Study Center, "Cheating in School."
57. Quoted in Sharon Jayson, "Dishonesty Was on Display Everywhere," *USA Today*, December 27, 2012, p. 02D.
58. Quoted in Jessica Lahey, "'I Cheated All Throughout High School,'" *Atlantic*, December 2013. www.theatlantic.com.
59. Lahey, "'I Cheated All Throughout High School."
60. Quoted in Keilman, "New Technology Lets Students Cheat More than Ever."
61. Leanna Landsmann, "Student Doesn't Understand Why Plagiarism Is Cheating," *Nashville Tennessean*, June 4, 2014. www.tennessean.com.
62. Quoted in Landsmann, "Student Doesn't Understand Why Plagiarism Is Cheating."
63. US Anti-Doping Agency, "Statement from USADA CEO Travis T. Tygart Regarding the U.S. Postal Service Pro Cycling Team Doping Conspiracy," October 10, 2012. http://cyclinginvestigation.usada.org.
64. Erika Christakis and Nicholas A. Christakis, "Harvard Cheating Scandal: Is Academic Dishonesty on the Rise?," *Time*, September 4, 2012. http://ideas.time.com.
65. Quoted in Medical News Today, "Violent Video Games Reduce Teens' Self-Control, Study Shows," Medical News Today, November 29, 2013. www.medicalnewstoday.com.

How Should Teen Cheating Be Addressed?

66. Jessica Lahey, "A Classroom Where No One Cheats," *Atlantic*, December 2012. www.theatlantic.com.
67. Yee, "Stuyvesant Students Describe the How and the Why of Cheating."
68. Quoted in Drew Keller, "Teacher, Student Groups Work to Design New Cheating Policy," *Paly Voice* (Palo Alto High School, Palo Alto, CA) December 19, 2013. http://palyvoice.com.
69. Quoted in Noguchi, "Among Many Teens, Cheating Is Part of School."
70. Pope, interviewed by Walker, "What Can Be Done About Student Cheating?"
71. Pope, interviewed by Walker, "What Can Be Done About Student Cheating?"
72. Ehrlich and Fu, "Cheating in Schools and Colleges."
73. Quoted in Richard Pérez-Peña, "Studies Find More Students Cheating, with High Achievers No Exception," *New York Times*, September 7, 2012. http://mobile.nytimes.com.
74. Quoted in Novotney, "Beat the Cheat."
75. Quoted in Novotney, "Beat the Cheat."
76. Quoted in Novotney, "Beat the Cheat."
77. Quoted in John K. Waters, "From Texting to Plagiarism, How to Stop High-Tech Cheating," *THE Journal*, September 9, 2013. http://thejournal.com.
78. Quoted in CBS San Francisco, "Leaked Questions at San Jose Schools Delay Standardized Test Results," July 19, 2012. http://sanfrancisco.cbslocal.com.
79. Sarah Togo, comment on Annie, "Ban Smart Phones in High School," Palo Alto Online, August 30, 2013. www.paloaltoonline.com.
80. Lahey, "A Classroom Where No One Cheats."

List of Illustrations

Index

Note: Boldface page numbers indicate illustrations.